the

Song of Songs

the
Song of Songs

G. I. WILLIAMSON

P&R
PUBLISHING
P.O. BOX 817 • PHILLIPSBURG • NEW JERSEY 08865-0817

Contents

Preface

The sermons that make up this study of the Song of Solomon were first preached to the Silverstream congregation of the Reformed Churches of New Zealand. It was my privilege, for some eleven years, to serve as the pastor of this remarkable fellowship of believers. Many of the older members were people who had come to New Zealand from the Netherlands, after the second World War. Most of the rest were their "second generation" children.

One of the things that these immigrants brought with them was a strong desire to uphold and maintain their Reformed heritage. And central to this is the conviction that all Scripture is inspired by God and profitable for the Lord's people. There was, therefore, no hesitation at all on the part of the elders of this church when it was suggested that I present an entire series of sermons on this neglected book of the Bible. And in my half-century of experience in the ministry I still look back on that series of sermons as unique. Through the entire series, the eyes of the people were riveted on their preacher. You could hear a pin drop in the auditorium. And everyone—from eight to eighty—was there to hear these sermons. I cannot adequately express the sense of wonder that I felt in preaching these messages. And the response was truly amazing. Right away it was suggested that these sermons be published. But how was this to be accomplished since I did not write these sermons out in full and didn't have time to do it.

The answer came when Yvonne van Maastricht—now Mrs. Yvonne Walraven—volunteered to transcribe these sermons. They read pretty much as they were spoken. And I am happy to take this opportunity to express my appreciation to her.

My one desire is that these sermons may also be a blessing to you as you read them.

1

Getting the Right Perspective

Song of Solomon 1:1

The text for this sermon is found in the Song of Songs in one short statement in verse 1: "The song of songs, which is Solomon's."

I can't help but wonder how many of you have ever heard a series of sermons on the Song of Solomon. I know that I went to church all my life—from the time I can remember anything, I remember going to church on the Lord's day—and I never heard any sermons on the Song of Solomon until I preached on the book myself. In my early ministry in the Orthodox Presbyterian Church in New England, I said one time that the whole Bible is the Word of God, and we should not be afraid to preach on any part of it, and I'm willing to do it. And what do you think happened then? Right away somebody said, "Okay, preach on the Song of Solomon." I can understand why preachers tend to shy away from it—because it's not easy to preach on a book about sex and marriage. It's especially difficult when you face a whole congregation of people of different ages. But I had to keep my word, and I'm glad I did!

You know in ancient times they had a saying that a man shouldn't even read this book until he's thirty years of age. Well, you laugh, but I think that they probably had things better under control in that culture than they do today. Like it or not, we live in an age when everybody knows so much about sex that it's probably a wise thing to stop talking about it once in a while. We are living in a sex-saturated and sex-dominated culture. And you know the result of it hasn't been very good. When half of the marriages end in tragic ruin, you can see that there's something radically wrong. But that's a very good reason for preaching on this book of the Bible because it would be sheer folly and stupidity to withhold the light of God's holy Word on this sacred subject, if it would help us at all in our culture and day, and I believe that it most certainly will.

And so, God helping us, I want to take you on a journey through this wonderful book of the Bible as we seek to understand from it what God says about love, sex, and the relationship of the sexes, and marriage that has his divine approval. And so by way of introduction let me point out to you first of all that this book, the one book of the Bible that is devoted wholly to this subject, is poetry. It is a song; it's not a technical sex manual, which is so very popular in American culture today. No, it's poetry, and I think that is a very significant thing in itself. When I left New Zealand, they were just bringing sex education into the schools, and many Christian parents were very much concerned because they saw this as another threat to their children. And, I think, rightly so. The parents realized that the whole approach to sex in the sex education being proposed to the high schools would have been quite different from the way in which it is presented in the Bible. You can present all the facts of life, all the details of the mechanism of sex, in a very cold and clinical way, with disastrous results. But if you come to see it in the framework of poetry, the way God puts it, and integrate it with all life, that is a very different thing.

Young people today know so much about sex anyway that I'd be the last person in the world to stand up here and try to tell them anything about it from the technical point of view. I was sitting one day in my study in New Zealand, and I was wishing I had a copy of the Encyclopedia Britannica, and I read in the local paper that there was one for sale, of all places, over at the high school. They had two, and they didn't need two—they wanted the money to buy something else—so I made a beeline over there, and I got that whole Encyclopedia Britannica for sixty dollars. And I took it home and began to use it with profit, but one day I noticed that in that encyclopedia there were some transparencies that showed the whole physiology of male and female, and they were the most worn-out pages in the Encyclopedia Britannica. The young people in that high school knew everything they could find out about the mechanism of the human body and sex. And that's what I'm talking about—we can't really have any doubt that the young people know it all from that standpoint, but do they understand the poetry of love?

The very encyclopedia that I just mentioned in its article on man had this to say: "The fragmentation of knowledge as it touches the subject of man appears to have gone very far. We have discarded eternal man"—and by "eternal man" the encyclopedia means the old integrated, Christian view of what man is in the cosmos—that has been discarded and we've cut him into pieces. Now that's true. No generation knows any more about the human "I" than today's, but the modern generation doesn't know where the "I" came from. No generation knows as much about the fine details of the God's creation, but it doesn't know where that creation came from. It doesn't understand the reality of man as a divinely created image-bearer of God. And that, also, is largely our problem when it comes to sex. And that is why the Bible uses poetry, not prose, to teach us about this holy subject, because true love and sex and marriage are poetry more than they are prose. It's more like a symphony than a factory—a factory is a production line; a symphony is something altogether different. And you know somehow I think all of us welcome that fact because down deep in our hearts we are the image of God, and God is the greatest artist and the greatest poet that there is. And he wants us to learn to think about love and sex and marriage in the context of something beautiful and poetic.

Now, the second thing that we learn from this opening statement is that the author of this book is Solomon. That's given a lot of people a lot of trouble. That's why a lot of commentators, and even a lot of conservative commentators, try to get out of it and find a way to say that somebody else, pretending to be Solomon, wrote this book. After all, they say, how could a man who had seven hundred wives and three hundred concubines write God's book about sex and marriage when he himself was such a terrible model? Talk about mechanized sex, that guy had it! Could he be the author of this book of the Bible? Come on, they say. And if he was the author when did he write it? Was it when he was a young man, just starting out, before everything went bad?

Well, there's an old proverb that says young men write poetry, and middle-aged men write proverbs, and old men write about vanity. While I haven't started writing proverbs yet, when I was a young man I used to write a little bit of poetry. That's a fact. I don't write it anymore and maybe that's a bad sign, but it is, I think, true that generally speaking this is the rhythm of life. Probably some of you men here might have written a little love poetry long ago, but it's also possible, it seems to me, that Solomon wrote this in his old age when he had learned what a fool he had been. You know the Bible says that this man was greatly loved of God even though foolish and outlandish women led him into sin—and it says that in a book of the Bible written much, much later by the inspired Nehemiah. And Nehemiah speaks about Solomon in such a way that I have no doubt that the man was, in spite of his failures and sin, a child of God. I don't believe that he would be the writer of a book of the Bible if that wasn't true.

And when you look at it that way, it doesn't really surprise you so much that God would use this man because, after all, who did God use to show us his own heart? The Bible says David was a man after God's own heart. The one who really shows us the heart of God more than anyone else in the Bible as a poet was David, and David was an adulterer and a murderer. Now that's a fact. And yet God chose that man's heart—of course, after he repented and got right with God again—to show us the depth of the emotions of a sanctified human heart. Well, why then should God not use a man who had seen it all, even from the wrong side, who when he was chastened of the Lord, repentant, and sanctified, could then write the greatest song in the world? There's not a reason on earth why that could not be. God took the greatest enemy of the church—Saul of Tarsus—and made him the greatest missionary of the cross. Why couldn't he then take the greatest sinner in the realm of sex that ever lived, if you like— Solomon, who had seven hundred wives and three hundred concubines—to write the greatest song that was ever written about love. Well, there's no way that we can be sure which view is true, but we do know that this was written by Solomon because it says so in the Bible, and I believe that also is something of great importance to us because it reminds us of the fact that the holiest part of God's holy Word is for sinners, and actually was written through sinners because there never was anyone that took up pen to write part of the Bible that was not like you and me—a sinner saved by grace. That's a wonderful thing. And if God could turn this man's heart right, and through his Spirit breathing through him write a poem like this, then God can take everyone one of us—whatever we may have done, and however great our sin may have been in the realm of sex and marriage—and he can make us to sing this song, also, to the praise and glory of his name.

One of the great marriages that I've read about in the history of the Christian church was the marriage of John Newton. Do you know anything about John Newton? Well, in his earlier life he was a slave trader—he went down to Africa to get slaves and took them all over the Western world, delivering them—and wherever he stopped he went to the prostitutes. Whatever city it was, off he went to the prostitutes and lived it up. And then God got hold of that man, and he was great in his repentance, truly renewed in his life, wholly converted in his heart, and then he got married. And they say one of the beautiful Christian marriages of that time was the marriage of John Newton, and his faithfulness and fidelity and devotion to his wife was a model for all the people that he served for many years as a faithful pastor in the church of God. Why not? Because God's kingdom has only converted, justified, adopted, and sanctified sinners—that's all there is in the Kingdom of God. And so it's a wonderful thing to me to know that this book was written by a sinner like Solomon who did everything wrong until he got right with God and then wrote this wonderful book of the Bible. So that's the second thing.

The third thing is that this is the greatest song in existence because the Hebrew phrase—"song of songs"—means that for sure. You know yourself whenever the Hebrew uses a phrase like that it's talking about the ultimate. What was the "holy of holies"? You know that the whole tabernacle was holy; everything in it was holy. But the holiest of the holy was that place where God's presence was manifested—that's why it was called the holy of holies. It was the supremely holy place in the tabernacle. Why is Jesus called the King of Kings? Well, it is because there is none like him. He is the ruler of all of the rulers of the earth. All the great and mighty and powerful of the earth are under the dominion of one, and only one, supreme King, and that is the Lord Jesus Christ. That's why he's called the King of Kings. And that's also why he's called the Servant of Servants, because no one ever stooped down and humbled himself in the way Jesus did. We can try to imitate him, but we will never equal him because Christ is the Servant of Servants. He is the one without equal.

Now, what that means is that Jesus Christ is our supreme and only Lord, and I believe that this opening statement proves beyond any question of a doubt that this song has to be about him in some way. You may know that back in the ancient synagogue and also in the early church and then again in the Puritan era, they took the Song of Solomon and made the whole thing into an allegory. Everything in it was taken to be a symbol of something entirely different from the symbol itself. We'll mention that as we go on through the book. But there was a tendency to try to interpret the book by making everything in it symbolic. The only trouble with that was that no two interpreters had the same idea about the meaning of that book because all of the symbols were differently interpreted by different people.

Now, in the modern era in which we're living, the tendency has been rather to take all the different parts of this book and see them only in a literal way, to look upon each and every one of these things only as something on the human level having to do with the relationship of man and woman.

My own view is that neither of these does justice to this book of the Bible because God himself—and we know this from the New Testament—made human marriage an image of the relationship of Christ to the church. Read Ephesians 5 where Paul says, "You've got to be subject to one another in the Lord." He says, "Wives, you have to be in subjection to your husbands." He says, "Husbands, love your wives," and he goes on speaking like that through the whole passage. And it's quite plain that he's talking very plainly and bluntly to husbands and wives and about their relationship with each other, and then all of a sudden he says, "This is a profound mystery—but I am talking about Christ and the church" (Eph. 5:32). Was he speaking about Christ and the church? Well, not directly, no. But indirectly, yes, because of this analogy that God himself has established between the relationship of Christ and the church and the relationship of marriage. The one is an analogy to the other.

After all, the Bible says all the treasures of wisdom and knowledge are hidden in Christ, and when Christ rose from the dead, he took his disciples right through the Bible and showed them that every book of the Bible, in one way or another, was about him. How, then, is this book about Jesus? Well, it's about Jesus because the ideal marriage is the marriage of Christ and the church, and the only way that you can ever get a hold of the ideal for your marriage is to understand the relationship between Christ and the church. Sometimes people say, "Do I really need all this doctrine in my daily life?" Well, friends, you certainly do. Nothing is more basic than understanding the doctrine of the church, the doctrine of Christ, and the doctrine of the union between Christ and the church in order to understand your own marriage, and what it ought to be, and what it can be. Of course, the two go together because the whole system of biblical truth is interrelated. And that's where so many go wrong when it comes to love and to sex and to marriage. So many people today try to deal with marriage without God, without Christ, without the church, and they are doomed to failure because there is no way that you and I will ever begin to know anything about the beauty of love and marriage without that great and only perfect model that is Jesus in his love for the church.

You might put it this way: The Song of Songs can only be sung by those who know the love of loves. And what is the love of loves? Here was a king, the greatest of all kings, sitting in his heavenly glory, and he looked down here on earth and he saw one that he would have as his bride. She wasn't very beautiful, but he set his heart upon her, and he would have her and none other. And once he had fixed his love upon her, nothing could ever distract him. And when you stop and think, you will see how many things there are that might have discouraged him, and yet he was willing to go down, to suffer, to descend into hell—all because of his love for his bride, the church. And the reciprocal love, the response love, of the church for Christ brings us to the other side of the matter. You see deep down in her heart the true church of Christ has a burning love for the Savior; nothing on earth, nothing in heaven or hell, will ever frustrate it or defeat it. And this, too, is the way it ought to be in our human love and marriage.

Now, where are you going to learn that? Have you got any other models that are that good? I've seen a lot of marriages—good, bad, and indifferent—but I've never seen any that are perfect. But that's our model, and that really is (and you'll see it as we go through this book) the model that comes to us through this great poem written by Solomon about his love for Shulamite maiden and her love for him. And you can't learn it anywhere else but the Bible. You know, beloved in the Lord, there is no such thing among sinful men as the perfect or ideal marriage. It doesn't exist, but there is such a thing in God's holy Word. It is the marriage of Christ and the church as it was imaged in this great idealization of Solomon and the Shulamite maiden. Whether that actually happened in his early life or was a reminiscence of his old age doesn't matter—it images the great love of Christ for the church, and what a wonderful thing it is to see what that image can do in the lives of people.

I remember years ago in our mission work I was going through a housing project talking to those who were willing to talk about the Lord, and I came across a young woman with four children, two from each of her previous husbands from whom she was now divorced. She wondered if there could be a future for her. You would have wondered too if you'd seen her. And yet, for about the last twenty-five years, she has been happily and faithfully married to a Christian husband. The marriage has endured. The children have grown up and have gone to a Christian college. And you have seen in that life what a glimpse of that model can do in somebody's life because she became one of the people of God, and God gave her a new beginning. And she came to see from the model of Christ's love for the church, and the church's love for Christ, what her life ought to be. And I believe God can do that for all of us, however far we may be from that standard of perfection, our God through this part of his Word can lift us up again and enable us to strive for the great goal of likeness to Jesus who loved the church and gave himself for it.

May God grant this to us as we study this book together. Amen.

2

The Beginning of True Love

Song of Solomon 1:2–2:7

You know, congregation, it's never an easy thing to understand what a poet is saying. You probably are aware of that. Sometimes you wonder, *Just what does the poet mean here?* When I was a university student many years ago, I majored in English literature. We studied many of the English poets, including, of course, one of the very greatest of all the writers in the English language, William Shakespeare, and to this day big books are being written by scholars trying to decide exactly what Shakespeare meant in certain places. And I discovered that even the experts don't agree, and that's true in every area of life.

So you not only have in poetry the problem of language, but when we're dealing with biblical poetry, we have the problem of another language, for this poem was written in Hebrew, and when you add to that the great differences between that time and our time, and that culture and our culture, you can see why I want to begin by saying that I don't pretend to have the last word on everything in the Song of Solomon. And I don't claim that I can fully explain every expression in this book. That's one reason why I think it is wise to expound a book like this in larger blocks of material so that we really get the drift of it and pick up the thread of what's unfolding in it. If we approach the book in this way, I believe we can be certain of its central teaching. Some of the details may indeed remain obscure, but I believe the main ideas that are being expressed are perfectly clear and certain. So what I want to do first of all is to try to expound this section of God's Word for you, and then in the concluding part of my message draw certain conclusions. So let me invite you to have your Bibles open as we look at this passage together. And as we do, I want to draw your attention to seven things that I believe are quite clear in this passage.

The first is that the poem begins with the words of this young woman who fell in love with the writer Solomon. This is evident from the gender of the pronouns in that passage: "Let *him* kiss me with the kisses of *his* mouth" (1:2), and so it goes on down to where she says, "My mother's sons were angry with me" (1:6). And then in the eighth verse of this passage, the first speaker is further identified when she is addressed by whomever—it's a kind of rhetorical, dramatic question addressed to the speaker up to that point—"If you do not know, most beautiful of women," then do this and so on. Now, we don't know who this girl was originally—what her name was, what family she came from, what tribe; it's obvious, however, that she comes from a humble station in life because she even had to do a man's work out in the vineyard. "Do not stare at me," she says, "because I am dark" (1:6). And why is she dark? "I am darkened by the sun. My mother's sons were angry with me and made me take care of the vineyards" (1:6) From his earliest days, Solomon must have been surrounded by a bevy of beautiful women; at least, beautiful in terms of that day and that culture. They were probably pampered women who had milky white skin and all of the latest cosmetics. In contrast to this, this country girl feels herself to be at a great disadvantage. She's dark, overexposed to the sun, and because of all the hard work she's had to do out in the family vineyard, her own vineyard—which I take to be a figure of expression denoting her own beauty— she has been forced to neglect. It is this girl who longs for the love of the exalted ruler of Israel. It is this girl who has set her heart on the king of Israel.

The second thing that is clear from the passage is that her greatest beauty is the beauty of her character, which shines out in her virtues. For her, love is not a game; it is not a series of clever flirtations, as it no doubt was for many in the court of the king. No, she has fixed her heart on the king and longs for his embraces. And you will notice that she does so not just because he is dashing and handsome, but also because of the quality of his person, for she says, "Your name is like perfume poured out" (1:3). Now we do know that in biblical times a name was very significant. A name wasn't just something you looked up in a book until you found something that sounded good and then gave that name to the child. In the Bible, a name was a real revelation of the person, and in Solomon's case his name was his fame. He was known throughout the world in that day as the wisest man in the world, because God had given him, had endowed him with, true wisdom. And that phrase, "Your name is poured forth like ointment," is the same as saying your reputation is truly wonderful and beautiful. It summarized what he really was. The word *Solomon* means "peace of God" and that's what really did shine out of his character and person in the day that he was a young ruler over Israel because of his God-given wisdom.

And this is just as important to her as his kisses. She wants his kisses, the kisses of his mouth, but she also greatly values the quality of his character. And you can see that in verse 3 and again in verse 4, when she says it is only right that they adore this man. "No wonder the maidens love you!" she says, right after saying, "Your name is like perfume poured out." And again she says in verse 4, "How right they are to adore you!" When a person is not only good to look at, but truly excellent in every respect, then you can appreciate the fact that many other people are also drawn to admire, respect, and even love that person.

The third thing that we see in this passage is that this girl has a respect for the God-given role of male and female. More and more today in our culture, women are talking about being liberated as women. What does it mean—"women's liberation"? Well, it means that they don't want to accept any more the role that God has given them. A lot of people think that if you have a role of subordination, that makes you unequal, but that's not true. Christ subordinated himself to the Father, but we know that he was equal with the Father. And so the idea that role subordination means less glory and honor is not true. And this girl did not want something other than the God-given role appointed to her sex, but she heartily embraced it, for you'll notice that she wants him to take the initiative. Let him kiss me, she says. Take me away with you, she says. Let the king bring me into his chambers. All the way through this passage we read little expressions that clearly reveal the fact that she desires this man to take the initiative and be her leader as well as her lover.

Right there you can see the fourth thing, namely, that she has a big problem. How can a country girl, with all these apparent disadvantages, hope to have a chance with a man sought by so many women? You women will probably appreciate that problem—you want a man, and he's desired by a hundred other women, what chance do you have? I think she's expressing this thought in verse 7: "Tell me, you whom I love, where you graze your flock and where you rest your sheep at midday. Why should I be like a veiled woman beside the flocks of your friends?" It's a way of expressing, "How can I meet that man without doing something that is contrary to my own moral principles?"

Some commentators say that in verse 8 you have friends speaking. That's the way the translators of the New International Version have put it down. But that word *friends* is entirely the work of modern translators. It's not in the Hebrew. We aren't sure this was said by friends. Maybe it was an editorial comment by Solomon himself, a kind of an aside in which he expresses beforehand a kind of foreknowledge he has of the situation. But in the last analysis, it doesn't make any difference—it's really a divine rhetorical question. God is the one who says, "If you don't know, most beautiful of women, then follow the tracks of the sheep; you stick to what you're doing and you'll be all right." And that is my view of the matter. It is a way of saying, You don't have to invent some artificial method of meeting this man. You just stick to what you're doing. You just be content with your lowly status, and God will take care of the rest. You see, she was wrong in thinking she would lose out because she was different, because she was in a lowly station. For the truth is that Solomon had already noticed her and had noticed her precisely because she was not like all the rest.

He expresses that in a very unusual way when he says, "I liken you, my darling, to a mare harnessed to one of the chariots of Pharaoh" (1:9). Now, I can't prove it, but I think that what that means is this. Usually hitched up to the chariots of Pharaoh were stallions, and don't forget that Solomon was a horse lover. Archaeologists have dug up the remains of the stables of Solomon, and he had more horses than you could believe. And if that man saw a whole line of chariots with fifty stallions and one mare, you can depend on it: he would have noticed that fact. And he is saying that this woman stands out in contrast to all those other women just as much as that mare would among the stallions of Pharaoh. And, you know, I think there is a little of that in all of us. A modern poet has even expressed the same thing. When it comes to the natural and the artificial which would you rather have?

> Henceforth I will not set my love
> On other than the country lass,
> For in the court I see and prove
> Fancy is brittle as the glass.
> What though in silver and in gold
> The bonny lass be not so brave
> Yet are her looks fresh to behold
> And that is it that love doth crave.
> Fair fall the petticoat of red
> That veils the skin as white as milk,
> And such as would not so be sped
> Let them go coy the gowns of silk.
> Keep, ladies, keep for your own turns
> The Spanish red to mend your looks,
> For when the sun my Daphne burns
> She seeks the water of the brooks,
> And though the musk and amber fine
> So ladylike she cannot get,
> Yet will she wear the sweet woodbine,
> The primrose and the violet.

Give me Daphne any day! You see, she's got that natural beauty, that unadorned beauty that God gives a lovely woman.

So while she's pining away for Solomon, constantly thinking about him, he's already thinking about her even before
she knows it, already wanting her for his possession. Now, in
those days they didn't have 24-hour deodorant that you used
to smell good all day long. In those days, the ladies wore a
thing around their necks with some herbs inside a little bag
and that was nicely hidden away where it would always give
off a fragrant smell. And that's what she's talking about in
verses 12–14. She is saying that her thoughts of this man are
with her like a sweet perfume twenty-four hours a day. Have
any of you ladies ever fallen in love and found that this was
true? Twenty-four hours a day, and you were thinking of that
guy. Is that true? I think it is.

> My lover is to me a sachet of myrrh
>   resting between my breasts.
> My lover is to me a cluster of henna blossoms
>   from the vineyard of En Gedi. (1:13–14)

The very nicest perfume that you can get comes from the
vineyards of En Gedi, and that's what her thoughts all day
long about this man really are. What a sweet aroma is the
aroma of love.

Now the fifth thing is the fact that the language of love
is the same in all generations. However many people speak
there from verse 15 on, and wherever you make the divisions—and I'm not sure that all of them made by the translators are right, yet we know that some, at least, are because
of the gender of the verbs and nouns—one thing is sure, and
that is the fact that in every culture, in every generation, and
in every language the talk of love is pretty much the same.
"How beautiful you are, my darling!" (NKJV: "Behold, you
are fair, my love!") Have you ever heard that, you ladies? "Oh,

how beautiful! Your eyes are doves." [NKJV: "Behold, you are fair! You have dove's eyes."] "How handsome you are, my lover!" [NKJV: "Behold, you are handsome, my beloved!"] (1:16). Have you ever heard that? That's the language of love, and if you've never spoken like that at some time in your life, then Cupid has not hit the bull's eye where you are concerned. But if you have spoken like that at some time in your life, you know exactly what is going on in this passage. You don't have to be an expert in interpreting every Hebrew word to see that. She has become to him the most beautiful thing in the world, and he has become to her the world's most handsome and eligible bachelor.

And you know something—that always happens when this is going on. Suddenly the self-esteem and morale of that girl begins to zoom up higher and higher. At the beginning, she was rather self-conscious, for she said, "Don't stare at me because I'm dark. I'm sunburned. You've got to make allowances for my appearance." But after she's heard him say a couple of times, "You're beautiful, my darling! Your eyes are doves," then she says, "I am a rose of Sharon, a lily of the valleys" (2:1). I'm not so bad, she says. Now she's not claiming to be number one. Those flowers are rather modest, but they are beautiful, and she knows she's beautiful now—he's told her. Wouldn't that convince her if he's told her? And so she is now more self-conscious, but at the same time more confident, of her appearance. And I believe that this is always what happens in love, and it seems to me, by the way, that not only does she think she is more beautiful, but she really is. I've noticed that in my own children—when they fall in love and move toward marriage, they seem to get more beautiful. It's a fact, isn't it? A fact of life—something begins to radiate out of their personality.

Well, the result of all this is, and this is my sixth point, that she's already sure that she wants this man as her husband. And you can see that in 2:3–6. She says,

> Like an apple tree among the trees of the woods,
> So is my beloved among the sons.
> I sat down in his shade with great delight,
> And his fruit was sweet to my taste.
>
> He brought me to the banqueting house,
> And his banner over me was love.
> Sustain me with cakes of raisins,
> Refresh me with apples,
> For I am lovesick.
>
> His left hand is under my head,
> And his right hand embraces me. (NKJV)

Already she is expressing mentally her desire for the most intimate relationship with this man. And let us say the Bible isn't prudish about sex. It doesn't see it as something strange, something evil, or something to be ashamed of. It's a natural thing, when this is happening, to be sick with love. It doesn't mean sick *of* love; it means sick *with* love. Have you ever seen a lovesick girl? Have you ever been a lovesick boy? Well, there is such a thing. And yet at the same time we must not overlook the fact that she feels this in the context of respect for his person. You can see this from two things in this passage. First of all, she honors his headship, and her love is not only sexual desire. It is also oriented to his character, for she says, "I sat down in his shade with great delight, and his fruit was sweet to my taste" (2:3 NKJV).

Now, what does that mean? It means this: a godly man has stability. His character is nourished by deep roots. And there's something about him—a strength of character and so on—that makes her willing to rest under his shadow. And every woman ought to be able to see that kind of character in the man she falls in love with. It's very dangerous to fall in love with a man of whom you cannot say "I can sit under that man's shade." If you can't say that, better stop and look again.

And the second thing is "his banner over me is love" (2:4). Now, what does that mean? If you were ever in the military service, you'll know what a tremendously important thing a banner is. In some of the military units of the United States Army, there are banners that have served since Civil War times, and it's an honor to serve under that banner. When you go into battle, and you go into war, you are sometimes called upon for extraordinary feats of courage, and you would never in this world do it if you were just following your own inclinations, but you look at that banner and think of what it stands for and the honor of your nation, and you say, "I'll do it." That banner calls out a response that otherwise wouldn't be there. Well, she says, "His banner over me, his power to command me, his power to have headship over me, is love." And you find that right through the Bible. A man's headship has got to be based on love. It's what we call loving leadership. And if a man loves his wife, he can lead her. It doesn't mean it will be easy, but it can be done. And if a man loves his wife, and she's like this girl, she can submit to it, too, because the banner will be love. She might not always want to do what he says to do, but if she knows he really loves her—and there's no question about that—she'll say, "I don't really feel like doing it, but I will. He loves me, and I'll do it. His banner over me is love."

And the third thing that's very clear in this passage is that she does not want to anticipate the blessing of complete union with this man, her lover, prior to the time of God's approval. She says, "Daughters of Jerusalem"—that is kind of a rhetorical address to all the other women in Israel—"I charge you by the gazelles and by the does of the field: Do not arouse or awaken love until it so desires" (2:7). That's a way of saying, "Don't try to stir up the fires of sexual passion until God himself gives his approval." You see, right here is where our whole generation has gone completely wrong. The sexual side of the relationship between a man and a woman has been drawn out of the context that God put it in. There's so much sexual stimulation today, and even evangelical Christians— and even whole denominations—are tending to yield ground in this area and say, "It's all right. You don't really have to wait till you get married." But you do because that's what the Bible says. You don't have a right to another person's total love until God says so, and God says so in the bonds of marriage. And she knew that, and she knew that the divine way is the right way, that God's way is the blessed way, and so she said, "Daughters of Jerusalem, I charge you, don't do anything to tempt me or to spoil the progress of God-ordained love. Wait until the right time ordained by him."

Now, as I say, there are other things in this passage that perhaps I can't explain, but those things, I believe, are perfectly certain. And I believe they teach us three very important principles that I would like to leave with you tonight. The first of which is that *we always need to keep life in balance*, and in this case that means we have to do justice to the physical side, but also the covenantal side of marriage. Sometimes in the Christian church in the past, the physical side has been almost denied. I can't remember as a young person, growing up in the church, that I ever heard anything from the pulpit about sex and marriage. And that's one of the reasons we are in the mess we are today. The previous generation was squeamish about sex in the ministry of the Word of God. That's a fact, and it can't be denied, and so there's been a reaction against it—quite understandably. God made women beautiful, and that's not an accident. God made sex, and that's not an accident. And God gave this mighty power that draws people together in sexual attraction, and that's not wrong. But it becomes wrong when, as in our culture today, it becomes all important and is separated from the context in which God has put it, the context we've seen unfolding here in this beautiful account of the love of Solomon and this young woman.

And this means we must always do justice also to the aspect of character. Anyone who separates sex from character is asking for an awful lot of trouble. Physical attraction was there, she doesn't deny it. She desires—let's be honest—to be in bed with this man. That's a fact. But not without the other things, not without being sure he's the kind of man she can also live, for a lifetime, under the shade of, whose headship and leadership she can always respect and abide by. She looked, in other words, also at the character, at the name, and God wants us to instruct our covenant young people that this is absolutely vital. That's why so many marriages are going down the drain today—people only look at sex, and then after their marriage they start to look at character. And just look at the results. You can't do it. You've got to look at both. Don't marry somebody who isn't sexually attracted to you and attractive to you—of course not—but don't marry somebody until you're absolutely sure he has the character that you really want to be subject to, or if you're a male, the character of a woman who really is willing to be subject to you in the Lord as she ought to be. Now that's the first principle.

The second principle is what I would call *the danger of things artificial*, and what a danger this is today in our culture. The model that many young people have today is the movie star and the pop idol, an absolutely devastating and destructive model. There's no character there; none of the foundational building blocks for a happy marriage. You can have sharp-looking clothes and a very dashing appearance, and that can lead you into one disaster after another. Don't make as a model for anything in your life a person whose own life demonstrates disaster in the area of marriage. You remember this young woman, and you remember the wise Solomon who out of all the women in the kingdom picked that girl who had character, for that's exactly what he did. He wasn't impressed by the latest style and hairdo; he was impressed by inner beauty of a tranquil and godly heart.

I remember in one congregation of mine there were two young people who fell in love and wanted to get married. And their parents were absolutely against it! "These kids are too young to get married," they insisted. That was the end of the discussion for the parents. Well, they were young, maybe a little too young to get married, but they were like these too young people here in the Song of Solomon. She was a very simple, unadorned, naturally beautiful person, and he was a really godly young man. They were both real Christians. They met at one of the youth camps, and they wanted to get married. And the thing that really impressed me was that they were godly in it. And I began to say, "No sir, this is not right."

The Westminster Larger Catechism says one of the sins against the seventh commandment is *undue delay* of marriage. Did you know that? Making young people wait too long is not right, provided the character is there. Well, they had these essentials, so I went to their parents and began to oppose them. I said, "You'd better wake up, or you're going to be the cause of disaster with your own children. Now they're both committed Christians, they're both godly—you don't have a biblical right to oppose their marriage because there isn't any arbitrary age in the Bible. The Bible doesn't say you have to

31

have eight years of higher education before you get married."
Well, they finally saw the light and went along with it, and I
heard later that this young couple are still doing wonderfully
today. They were married quite young, but they had what it
takes. We've got to be on our guard against going along with
what everybody else does. We've got to get back to biblical
principles. There's no reason in the world why they shouldn't
have the right to marry just because they didn't match somebody's arbitrary idea of how old you have to be, not when
they have the character. Now I don't mean you young people
should rush out and get married right away just to prove that
you can do it young. That's not my point. My point is we
must avoid the artificial, and going along with everything that
everybody else does.

And finally, the third and last principle is to remember that
we always see in these things the image of something higher
and we need to remember that the great model that we must
always build our marriages on, and our love affairs too, is the
model of Christ and the church. And there are two things I
want to say about that. First of all, *can you imagine Christ being
attracted by anything artificial in the church?* There he is in glory
with all the angels—why in the world would he set his heart
upon us down here in this world of sin? It's not because of
anything artificial, I can tell you that for sure. That's why the
Reformed church was right when it set aside all that artificial
rubbish—the candles and the crosses and the robes and the
man-made ceremonies—and went back to plain, simple worship. They wanted to be the kind of wife that the Lord takes
delight in—his beautiful bride. Anything artificial should
always be banished from the church of Jesus Christ because
the beauty of the church of Christ is in her humility and simplicity, and as soon as she starts putting on paint and all kinds
of artificial beauty aids, she becomes very displeasing to the

Lord. Right there you see the difference between Rome and the Reformation. And we ought to remember that.

The second thing under this point is that the church sometimes becomes impatient and tries to take the initiative away from her Lord, and that is always wrong. We must be patient. We must wait for the Lord to take initiative. We desire the day of the consummation, the great wedding feast of the Lamb, but that will only come when he is ready. We must respect his headship and patiently wait as we pray, "Come, Lord Jesus, come quickly," without trying to anticipate the glorious day of his coming. The model for us is the way in which Christ deals with the church, and the way in which the church acknowledges his headship.

And now may God apply these lessons to our hearts.

Amen.

3

Getting to Know You

Song of Solomon 2:8–3:5

Congregation of the Lord Jesus, in the last sermon we saw how this young girl from the nation of Israel, lowly of origin, met the king. And she saw that he was not only handsome, but a man endowed with the wisdom of God, and she desired him; and he, because she was so different from all the rest, also desired her. You remember, too, that she accepted the God-ordained role that he has given the woman. She wanted him to take the initiative, and she wanted to sit under his shade and be under the banner of his love. It was precisely because of these qualities that the king noticed her and began to seek and desire her. And so there began this process of falling in love in which she began to feel that he was the kind of man she could gladly submit to, and he that she was the object of his desire. But then you'll remember that she added that very significant statement, "I adjure you, daughters of Jerusalem"—which means "I call upon you to solemnly swear in faithfulness to our covenant God"—"that you won't do anything to arouse, to stimulate this love until its time has come." Well, now we're going to look at the second phase of this relationship, something that we commonly call *courtship*, and I want to deal with it under two basic headings. The first is the seven certain things that we find in this passage and then the simple lessons that we can learn from it.

What we see in this passage is the story of the beautiful courtship between Solomon and the Shulamite maiden. And the first thing that is quite obvious is *a growing intensity in their love for one another*, or to put it in modern lingo, they really are "stuck" on one another. Now, the language of every age is rather unique, but I think even today we can really sense what is being said in these first few verses. "Listen!" she says, "My lover! Look! Here he comes, leaping across the mountains, bounding over the hills" (2:8). Did you ever hear of anything like that today?

Let me try to draw you a picture. I've noticed that when young ladies fall in love, they suddenly have a very different attitude toward the telephone. Before my daughter fell in love, if the phone rang, well, you could answer it, thanks. She couldn't be bothered. But, my, how that changes when you fall in love. The phone rings, and like a bullet she's down there to answer the phone. And does he really come leaping over the mountains? Well, we wouldn't say that today, but he zooms over the mountains, either in his car or, as was common in New Zealand, on his motorcycle. And the extravagance of the language is really quite fitting when you realize what's going on here, as there is an extravagance in the way they act, also. I remember a very wonderful man in the New Zealand church—he was an elder for many years and also served as the stated clerk of their General Synod. He told me what it was like when he fell in love in Holland with his dear departed wife. He was a very young man, and he worked hard all day long, and then he said, "You know, I didn't think a thing about it. I walked several miles just to see her for a few minutes. And when I got there I was so bashful and embarrassed, I hardly knew what to say. And then I walked all those miles back and I didn't even feel tired."

Well, that's the same sort of thing that's really put before you here in this picture. This fellow, too, is zooming over the hills, you might say, but when he gets there, he's a bit bashful—he stands behind the wall, he gazes through the windows, and he peers through the lattice. You know what that's like, don't you? You don't quite have the courage to show yourself, but you are there to get a sight of her. You see, the fundamentals of life haven't changed very much in all these generations.

The second thing you see for sure in this passage is that *they need to be alone with each other* because then the awkwardness fades away. Why are they so awkward and embarrassed? Well, it's because there's somebody else around, that's why. So right away he says, "Arise, come, my darling; my beautiful one, come with me" (2:13). Let's get out of here; let's go where we can be alone together, for that makes all the difference. As soon as they do that, the birds begin to sing and it's spring. See, the winter is past, the rains are over and gone, flowers appear on the earth and so on. You know, in the languages of all the nations of the earth this is the way that love is depicted. The poet John Clare put it like this:

> The Spring comes in with all her hues and smells
> In freshness breathing over hills and dells.
> The happy time of singing birds has come,
> And love in Nature's beauty finds a home.
> Among the mossy oaks now coos the dove,
> And every sound that meets the ear is love.

Now that's true, when you fall in love, there's nothing wrong with this world—it's beautiful, isn't it? You don't think about the things that aren't pleasant in the world when you fall in love. As one commentator put it, "Whenever any couple falls in love, it's spring. It doesn't matter if it's December—it's spring when they fall in love because their lives are fresh, and everything has a new perspective." John Milton, the great blind English poet who wrote *Paradise Lost*, described the relationship of Adam and Eve before the fall into sin like this: "With thee conversing I forget all time. All seasons, and their change, all please alike." In the springtime of love, there is an echo of the Paradise of God, because that's when man seems to be at one with nature. Milton was right—that's the way it was in the beginning.

The third thing that is quite sure in this passage is that *they have a great desire to know one another fully.* And here it's the man who talks about her shyness for a very good reason. You can imagine why—he's the king of Israel and she is what we would call a peasant girl, and she is getting into this romance. My, that would be difficult for her. She would feel shy, and it would be very hard for her to completely reveal her personality to him, and so he compares her to a dove in the clefts of a rock. Now, you all know that the Dead Sea Scrolls were found in a kind of cave way up on the side of the face of the rock. Well, in biblical times you might see a dove up there, but if that dove saw you, you know what she would do, don't you? She'd hide. If that dove saw you, she would hide herself away so you could hardly get a glimpse of her. My sister is a confirmed bird watcher, and with her binoculars she tries to get to a spot where the birds won't notice her, and then she zooms up on them, and she can watch what they're doing. But they didn't have binoculars in those days, and when you tried to get close enough to see what the doves were doing, they would hide. Well, she's a bit like that. Part of her personality—and the reality of who she is—is still hidden, but he wants that to come out. He wants her to show her face, and he wants to hear her voice because her voice is sweet. He wants her to talk and smile and all the rest of those things. And that was not easy for this country girl.

Now, girls if you're a little bit like that today, you're going to be in a very small minority, aren't you? I could even see a smile as soon as I said that, because I can just imagine what it's like with the average high school girl right here where we live. It's not like that at all, and what a pity it is—really what a pity. For to be a bit shy, not so fast that you've got it all figured out, is a good thing; it's a biblical, godly thing. Solomon could have had a hundred girls of the other kind—they called them concubines in those days—quite willing to have an affair that really didn't get very deep and didn't last very long, but that's not what he wanted—at least, at this point in his life he didn't. He wanted something that was really beautiful and patterned after God's ordinance, and for that you have to have a process of self-revelation until more and more you really do get to know one another, and that finally means complete knowledge of one another, body and soul, for a lifetime. That's what marriage really is: the disclosure to another person of who and what you really are. And that wasn't easy, and it takes time, and that's exactly why, no matter how outmoded it may be in the minds of young people today, courtship *is* biblical. Courtship is a gradual process by which two young people really get to know one another before they get too far in the matters of love. That's the third thing.

The fourth thing that is certainly clear here is this: *when you are in the midst of a courtship, you're going to have problems.* Does anyone here know of an exception to that? I don't believe so. As soon as you have a romance going, you're going to have problems. Not big ones like elephants, but little ones like foxes. And so Solomon says, "Catch for us the foxes, the little foxes that ruin the vineyards, our vineyards that are in bloom" (2:15). Now, you remember back in 1:6, this maiden spoke of her vineyard. She was speaking there about her love, which she had not yet given to a man, and here he's talking about their love for each other as it's beginning to develop and unfold in the process of courtship. And now he says these foxes come in and they spoil the vineyard. Now, what are these foxes? I believe they are irritations. She does something, and it really irritates him. Now, how can that happen when you're having a courtship and you're falling in love? But it does happen.

And I want to tell you something, it is a good thing it does happen. Really it is, because then you are going to learn the fact that you're falling in love with another member of the fallen human race. That's the only kind of human being that you will ever find in this world. You can't find a husband that isn't part of Adam's fallen race, and you can't find a wife that isn't part of Adam's fallen race, and that means that they are going to have faults! That is for sure. And what you've got to learn is that you will have to understand these faults, and you will have to learn to deal with these problems in a biblical way. That is one of the purposes of courtship: you have to learn to catch the little foxes; you have to learn how to deal with these irritations and problems; to learn how to handle the stressful situations without blowing up and doing sinful and wicked things.

When two young people would come to me wanting to get married, I made it a habit to observe them very carefully. I would seek to discern whether they were constantly arguing and never able to solve their problems. If they were, I would say to them, "I really don't think it would be wise for you two to get married because you haven't learned to handle your problems yet. And if you can't handle the little foxes, what are you going to do when the big ones come along because they will in marriage?" The big problems are later on; the little ones are while you're just getting to know each other, and if you can't handle the little problems and settle them in a biblical manner, with love and understanding, on the basis of biblical principles and discussion in which your Bible is your guide, then you're not going to make it. That's the fourth thing.

The fifth thing in this passage is that *there is a growing desire for total possession.*

> My beloved is mine, and I am his.
> He feeds his flock among the lilies.
> Until the day breaks
> And the shadows flee away,
> Turn, my beloved,
> And be like a gazelle
> Or a young stag
> Upon the mountains of Bether. (2:16–17 NKJV)

What she is saying here is that she desires total possession of him and desires to be totally possessed by him. And that also is definitely part of God's plan for the relationship we call love and marriage.

Today, there are those who talk about open marriage. They don't want to make that complete and total commitment; they don't want to say, "I, from now on, for better or for worse, am the possession of that person, and that's that. Nobody else has any rights to me any more—I belong to that person." A lot of people today are afraid of that. They see so many ruined marriages, and so they think that maybe it would be better to just have an open marriage, so that if, a year from now, things aren't going so well, they can walk right out of it. But God didn't make us that way. I knew a young man who was a member of a covenant family in New Zealand, and he thought he knew better than the Bible, and so he went out, and he shacked up with a girl. He thought, "Well, we'll just have an open marriage. We won't go through these vows. We'll just live together and see how it goes." And they loved each other—that's the remarkable part of it—but you know they weren't really happy. And do you know why they weren't happy? Because down deep each of them was a little anxious about the other person. They wanted to have possession of that person. And so finally one day they said, "We have to go and get married." And that's what they did; they got married. And after they made that total commitment, they began to be happy. You see, psychologically even, you can't live with that idea of an open marriage. It's contrary to human nature. God made you, and God made me, with an absolute need of total possession in marriage. So this whole modern idea of an open marriage is flagrantly in violation to the law of God.

But she doesn't possess him yet, and that's part of courtship, too. So the sixth thing we see is *the anxiety of unfulfilled desire*: "By night on my bed I sought the one I love; I sought him, but I did not find him" (3:1 NKJV).

Now, I'm not sure whether this was a dream or just her imagination. I tend to think it was a dream, but that doesn't matter as far as the main point is concerned. In any event, she had anxiety. And why did she have anxiety? Because she was afraid she might lose him. Now, if any of you older folks can remember back when you were courting, I'm sure you can remember when that happened to you. A moment came when you thought, "Wouldn't it be terrible if I lost him—if, after all, he didn't want me." So she gets up, either in fact or in dream, and goes around the city looking for him. And when the watchmen find her wandering around, she says, "Have you seen the one my heart loves?" (3:3), and then hardly had she passed them when she found him. And when she found him, she thought, "I'm not going to let this happen again," and so she says to herself, "I'm going to get him down home to meet mother." You see, that kind of solidifies the thing, that kind of ties it up. So she brings him there and has him meet her mother, and by doing so she knows that he's just that much more committed. So here again is something that's supposed to be out of date today, but I find that, psychologically, it's still very true.

Our youngest daughter for quite a while in her young life was not committed to Christ, and I noticed that she never liked to bring her boyfriends home. We had to keep asking, "Who is this fellow? Where does he live? What is he like?" and it was always from a distance. So we had to wonder. But when she became a committed Christian, do you know what she did? She grabbed her man and got him in a car and had him drive hundreds of miles to meet us. Now why? Because she wanted to sew the thing up, that's why. She didn't want to lose him, and she thought, "If I can get him down there to meet Dad and Mother, that will show that he really is serious, and besides I think they'll like him." And we did. We think a lot of him because of his Christian profession. It made all the difference in the world—family approval—and it's also a biblical part of courtship. It should never be left out of a Christian view of courtship.

And then finally the seventh thing is that *she remained firm in her decision: no sex until marriage.* And here you notice that she repeats that statement, "Daughters of Jerusalem, I charge you. . . . Do not arouse or awaken love" until the proper time has arrived (3:5). The modern view is "what difference will it make if we go ahead and have sex? We're going to get married anyway." But that's not the way it really is, because we don't really have possession of another person until there is a public declaration of that fact. Now a man might think, "I can go out and start preaching even though no one has yet officially declared that I have the authority to do it." Well, that's not true, he can't. And then some guy might say, "Well, I'm going to go out and be a traffic officer" before they give him his uniform and his badge, but that's not true; he can't do that. And you don't have a right to that other person until you've said before the whole world, and your partner has said before the whole world: "I belong to him, and she belongs to me; and everybody else is off limit." That's what marriage really is. It's a covenant contract. That's why premarital sex is condemned in the Bible, punishable in the Bible under the Law of Moses—not by death as an unpardonable or capital crime— but as a serious sin nonetheless. There was a fine that had to be paid to the father, which shows that it's really a violation of the honor of the family that is at stake. And this woman didn't want that; she wanted to do it God's way until the day that God himself said they belong to each other. Now that's the biblical pattern of courtship. What does it teach us?

The first thing it teaches us is that courtship—when it is lived out in the way we see it here—gradually leads, step by step, to total commitment and total, mutual possession. Do you remember the song from the well-known operetta, *The King and I*, called "Getting to Know You"? That's a pretty good portrait of what courtship really is.

I remember an interesting documentary about the ascent of Mount Everest. There was quite a group of men that made the long climb toward the peak. But it was only when they got to the highest camp, before the summit, that the one in charge decided which two men would make the final assault on the peak. Do you know why? He wanted to observe how they met all the tests up to that point, and those who really met the tests up to that point, they were the ones to make the assault on the peak. If young people today understood what a tremendous challenge marriage is, they would also want to go through a time of testing. We each need to test ourselves and the one that we think we want to marry. Only then can we can be really sure that together we can climb to the summit.

When I was a boy of eight or nine years of age, I was playing in a park one day. I don't remember why I went there, but I remember what happened. All of a sudden, I heard these two young people quarrelling, so I threw the ball in that direction and acted like I was chasing the ball, but really I was going over there so I could tune in to what they were saying. I listened for about three minutes and then turned away. I said to myself, right there and then, "Those two should never get married." It was already clear, even to a young boy, that they couldn't handle their problems. That's why courtship is so very important, and it's also a good reason why premarital sex is not only *wrong* but very *unwise*. You first need to know that the context of love and sex is something that's stable, firm, and solid. So you don't wake up and realize you are stuck with someone you wouldn't really *want* to be married to for the rest of your life.

And right here, again, you can see the beautiful analogy between the heavenly and earthly—the analogy between *our* marriages and the marriage of Christ and the church. You know the marriage feast of the Lamb of God and the church hasn't taken place yet—it's still in the future. The Bible tells us that there will be a great feast to celebrate the marriage of the Lamb and his bride. And sometimes we get a little anxious, and we'd like him to hurry up and speed things. But that's not God's wise way. He knows we need this time—shall we call it a time of courtship—in which we get to know the Lord in the way that we should. Now, if you want to be part of that marriage you ought to be doing everything you can to prepare for it. That's why you ought to be in God's house whenever you have the chance to hear the Word, and that's why you ought to be preparing for the coming of Jesus, being faithful in the things of God, because the day is coming when there will be a complete revelation of Jesus Christ. That's what the Bible says. And *then* we will know him even as he is, and we want to be sure that we're ready.

So, in a sense our very meeting here is part of this courtship process by which we get to know the Lord in anticipation of the glorious day when we will be with him forever.

May God give us the wisdom to do so.

Amen.

4

Lovers' Lib

Song of Solomon 3:6–5:1

Congregation, it was our Lord Jesus Christ who said to his disciples, "You will know the truth, and the truth will set you free" (John 8:32). So truth is the foundation of freedom. The number one thing you need to have to really be free is knowledge of the truth of God. And I hope that this will become very clear as we look tonight at this portion of God's holy Word.

We have been looking at this song of love in the Bible, and we have seen in it the pattern of falling in love, courtship, and now marriage. And we have been learning in this that God has his way for these things to take place, and that this is real freedom. Today in our society, as I hardly need to tell you, it is another view that prevails. If you love one another, it is said today, then it's all right—go ahead. Don't worry about a little thing like a marriage ordinance. But these young people that we meet in the Song of Solomon were wise. They understood that God knows more than we do, and that his is the good and right way.

And so this wonderful young woman—this Shulamite maiden that married Solomon—over and over, prior to her marriage, makes this tremendous statement: "I adjure you, daughters of Jerusalem, that you not arouse or stimulate love until the appointed time." And now she's taken her man home to meet her parents, and they're engaged to be married. And here at last, in our text for tonight, we come to the consummation of her desires. You will notice that there are really three major divisions in our text. The first—which comes in the last part of Song of Solomon 3—is what I would call *the official, or the public, ceremony of marriage*. The second—which follows after that—is what I would call *the beautiful ritual of sexual intimacy in marriage*. And the third—but by no means the least—is *the benediction that God places upon these two young people*. When you have those three things which God has appointed, *then* you really have freedom.

We begin, then, in 3:6–11, with the wedding of Solomon and the Shulamite maiden. And we know that this is what it is because it says so in verse 11. Now we have to admit, ladies, that it's a bit of a put-down for you, since in our culture it's the bride who gets all the attention, whereas here, in this marriage, it was Solomon. Now why was that? Well, one reason could be the simple fact that he was the king. Even today—in Great Britain—if the titular head of the monarchy is a woman, and there is a marriage, she gets all the attention. If it's a man, then *he* is the one who gets it. So it may simply be the fact that he is the inheritor of the throne of David that he gets all the attention. Or it could be that in biblical times the headship of the man received more attention in these things than it does today. But whatever may be the explanation, one thing is quite certain, and that is the important thing—*there was a public ceremony of marriage*. And, by the way, the thing that his mother crowned him with was a wreath—a wedding wreath—not the crown which he wore as king. This was not a coronation ceremony, but a public ceremony of marriage.

I want to emphasize this because many today say the ceremony doesn't matter. If anything has really become quite prominent in our day and generation, it's the idea that an official public ceremony of marriage (like a traditional one you have in the church) is really not very important. What really matters in marriage—it is said—is the private, intimate side where two people really do love one another. Well, of course, marriage does involve that side, and I will even acknowledge that the ceremony in and of itself does not a marriage make. I remember very well one of my seminary classmates who got married in a public ceremony, and I didn't know anything of the sort had happened, but many years later I heard that marriage was annulled because for some reason—and I haven't the slightest notion what it was—that marriage was never consummated in sexual union. So, finally, the wife went to the civil authorities and complained against her husband, and the wedding was annulled. You don't really have a marriage in the biblical sense without physical intimacy. But you can't say that the physical side alone is a marriage either, because you are not really married without the public ceremony.

It's a little like baptism. Now, of course you are aware that the water of baptism, by itself, will not save you. You could be baptized a hundred times and still perish forever. But anyone who says, "I don't need to bother with baptism" is very much mistaken, because it is an ordinance commanded by our Lord. His command was to go out into all the world to preach the gospel and to baptize everyone who received it. So, it is just not true that you can count on being saved without water baptism—because saying no to baptism is disobedience to the Lord Jesus. It is God's appointment, and faith is made known by its works. So the person who really has a proper place in the kingdom of God, under ordinary circumstances, is a person who is *outwardly* baptized with water and *inwardly* regenerated by the Holy Spirit, and both of them are very important.

And it's the same when it comes to marriage. Of course, the intimate and private is very important, but it is not the only thing that is important. According to the Bible, the public side is also important, and I can tell you why. When you enter into marriage, the way God has planned it and the way God has ordained it, you are really making a declaration, not only to the person you love in private, but to the whole world in public. You are saying, in effect, "Listen, world, from now on I'm off limits to you, and I belong to this woman only." And she is saying, "Listen, world, from now on I'm off limits to everyone else; from now on I'm the exclusive possession of this man." That's what the Bible means when it says a man is to *leave* his father and mother and *cleave* to his wife. It's not a private matter only; it's also a public thing that involves the honor of the families as well as the delight and joy of the two people.

What would you think of someone claiming to be a policeman who didn't have a uniform and didn't have a badge, and said, "Never mind about those outward things—they don't matter"? Of course they do. What would you say if the governor of your state said, "Never mind about all those vows of office and that sort of thing, I'm just going to be governor?" Well, if anyone tried that, I'm sure we would say, "No way; we don't want you for governor if you're not willing to take those vows. You can stay home and we'll have somebody else as governor." These public things are very important, and we are not at liberty to ignore or deny them. What would you think if somebody got up here to preach who had never been ordained by the church? He might say, "I don't need ordination. I have the Holy Spirit, I have the knowledge and a fluent tongue, so I can preach. Ordination doesn't matter." But it does matter. What would you think if you went to the doctor and he said, "Well, I've never been to medical school, I don't have a diploma, but I know about medicine and that's all that counts"? No! It's not all that counts. Of course it isn't, and it's the same when it comes to marriage. It is very important to have a public ceremony in which you declare to the world on the one hand, and to that person you marry on the other, your covenantal commitment. And so right here in the great song of love—in 3:6-11—you have this statement about a public ceremony. We don't have to do everything they did in that day and generation, or imitate everything in that culture, but this is one of the important facts of God's revelation in this book.

Now the second thing you have in this book is what I would call *the tender ritual of sexual intimacy in marriage*. It is to this that I now direct your attention.

When I was a young fellow, I was a jazz musician, and a friend and I were once playing in a band in a Masonic lodge. We were upstairs in this building and saw a beautiful set of chimes that we coveted. I said, "Bill, wouldn't it be great if we could have those chimes." And he said, "Yes, it sure would." So I said, "Why don't we take them." He said, "All right, we'll take them." And I said, "You go downstairs during intermission, and I'll throw them out the window to you. You put them in the car, and we'll have a set of chimes." And so, sure enough, when the intermission came, he went outside, and I tossed the chimes out the window. He caught them and put them in the car and not a thing was damaged. And we thought, "Wow! We're going to have fun with those chimes." But you know, when the job was over, and we went home, I said, "Why don't you take them, Bill." And he said, "No, you take them," and I said, "No, I don't want them either." You see, I was afraid somebody might ask where I got those chimes, and so I thought it would be better if Bill had them, but Bill didn't want them either, because he too was worried that somebody might find out that we stole them. So finally we said to each other, "Let's go and put them back," and that's what we did. You see, you can't be free if somebody's looking over your shoulder, or if you're looking over your shoulder to see if somebody's looking over your shoulder. That's not freedom. You think you're really going to enjoy it a lot, but it's not real freedom, and it's not really a pleasure. And if that is true with a set of chimes, surely it is a thousand times more so when it comes to one of God's greatest gifts to another person.

This young couple understood that, and so they waited until they had a right to each other, and the result was that they were really free. They had a license, you might say. When you get a driver's license, you can go out and drive your car. Yesterday you couldn't do it. Today you can. If you get a marriage license, and you have a wedding ceremony, you can go to bed with that person and it's perfectly all right, though yesterday it was not right at all. That is God's way, and when you do it that way you can be completely free—no bondage in it all.

And you can see that in the way Solomon praises his wife's physical beauty. Now, we don't do it this way today, but if you were living in Solomon's day and wanted to say that your wife was beautiful, you would say seven things—not eight, not six, just seven. In the Hebrew way of thought, seven really meant terrific, and so if you go through that list, you'll notice that he mentions seven, and exactly seven, of her beautiful characteristics. And he must have really thought about it, because he gives such a poetic description of each one of them. You can't do that when you're on the run, in the back seat of a car some place, hiding, and looking over your shoulder. It just doesn't work that way. And by the way, I think you'll notice that even though this is poetry, it's rather plainly sensual and sexual. Back in 2:17, this girl expressed the desire that one day her fiancé would be like a young gazelle or a stag on the mountains of Bether. And the word *Bether* means "separation," and I agree with the commentators who say that what she's really talking about there is what we today would call "cleavage," and you'll notice that in this passage when he describes the same thing, he's rather rhapsodical about it, for he speaks of the mountains of myrrh and incense. Now, my point is this. When the Christian church was too prudish to admit that God made the female of the species beautiful—and that sex is very exciting—it made a big mistake because it drove the whole thing underground where it didn't belong, and it pretended that this was not what it really is: one of God's good gifts that should be frankly acknowledged for what it is, but only within the bonds of marriage.

It is quite clear in this passage that this Shulamite girl was a virgin when she got married. And there are even some who argue, today, that this is a liability. It's just possible that some of you young people here in our congregation have heard that argument from some of your peers. And it's true, is it not, that if you are completely inexperienced and you enter into marriage, it won't be easy—in one day—to completely reveal yourself to another person. I believe that is really what's going on in that passage. Please open your Bibles and notice what it says. He says there in 4:8–9: "Come with me from Lebanon, my bride. . . . Descend from the crest of Amana . . . from the lions' dens and the mountain haunts of the leopards." He's talking about the fact that this girl is rather shy and reserved; she's even a little bit afraid, just as you would be afraid if you were near the dens of the lions or near the mountain haunts of the leopards. He's aware of this, and he's considerate of her feelings, and so he's saying to her, "You need to leave these fears behind because this is the day that you gave yourself to me. And in order to leave all those fears behind you have to be willing to trust me."

You know, the art of love isn't something you can learn in ten easy lessons, and that's because any two human beings are distinctively different from any other two. Every personality is distinctively different, and wise Solomon understood that. Because his approach was right, and he understood and was patient, it wasn't long before she was quite willing to reveal herself to him. She says, for the first time in the book, *"Let my beloved come to his garden and eat its pleasant fruits"* (4:16 NKJV). Always before in the book it was her garden, which she was keeping locked, but now it was *his* garden.

I read the testimony of a preacher who preached on this passage of the Bible, and when he finished and all the others had gone, there was a girl who came up to him, and she was crying and said, "Sir, I left my garden unlocked. Now, is there any hope for me? What can I do?" Well, he said, "Suppose you had a flower garden and somehow the gate was left open and the dogs came in and dug around and some of them walked over the flowers, what would you do?" She said, "I would lock the gate, then get the hoe and the rake and start cleaning up the garden." And he said, "That's exactly what you should do." And that's the really beautiful thing about our holy faith. God never lowers his standard. He never says wrong is right. Nobody will ever hear God say, "Fornication is all right; go ahead and don't worry about it." God will never say that. He has absolute standards, and "sin is any want of conformity unto, or transgression of, the law of God," and that's the way it will always be. But this same God is compassionate, and he says, "Though your sins are like scarlet, they shall be as white as snow" (Isa. 1:18). And he can make you a new creature in Christ, and we know this because the bride of Christ (and that is after all the great model upon which the whole book is based) is the church, and the church was not a garden locked. The church was a company of unworthy sinners whom Christ cleansed and renewed by his own precious blood and by the Word of his power.

And now, finally, please notice that last statement in 5:1. One version suggests that it's friends who say, "Eat, O friends, and drink; drink your fill, O lovers." And that's possible. But there is nothing in the Hebrew text that says this. It could be what we call an editorial comment. Maybe the one who speaks is the wind—that is the last antecedent noun. If you go back to 4:16, it's the wind that is addressed. So maybe it is the wind? But one thing is absolutely certain, whether it is the friends, or the wind, or an editorial comment, or the Lord God himself who speaks directly, ultimately this comment comes from God at the end of this beautiful process of falling in love, courtship, a public ceremony of marriage, and a consummation of marriage in sexual intimacy. Yes, it is God himself who says, "Eat, O friends, and drink; drink your fill, O lovers." Only in such a benediction of God is there total and complete freedom.

In our New Zealand church, we had a large young people's group, and we met once a month after the evening service for discussion. And I noticed a young couple that came that didn't look very happy, and by discreetly listening and asking a few questions, I found out the reason. They were living together as man and wife on the sly, and I think what they were really after was some clue or indication that maybe the church was willing to tolerate this. But I noticed that they didn't seem happy. No, they weren't happy, and the reason was that they weren't really free—not even free from their own conscience. So I began to talk to them about it. I said, "Do you know why you're not happy? It's because you're not free. And do you know why you're not free? It's because you can't be free without God's approval. Do you want God's approval?" "Oh yes," they both said at once. "Oh yes, we'd love to have God's approval." I said, "All right, no problem." I said to her, "You go home, tonight, to your mother's house and stay there, and then you make plans for a marriage. And then you get married, and then you'll have it. Stop this right now and do what God says from here on, and you will have God's blessing."

Now, it isn't every day that young people pay attention to words like that, but this time they did. She did go home, and they stopped it then and there. And not too long after they got married, and it was like turning lights on inside their faces, because they knew now they had made a public commitment and they had God's own approval and his benediction. And the last I heard they were still happily married out there in Australia; they moved across the Tasman Sea to Australia. Well, that's what I could call freedom. "Lover's liberation"—there it is. Are you young people interested in real freedom in the realm of sex? Well, there it is right here in God's Word—a proper courtship and marriage with God's approval.

And now let me say two things in conclusion from this portion of God's Word, and here's one of them that I think the church has to hear. And the first is the fact that *sexual love has its own value by God's appointment.* I emphasize this because there was a time in the church of God when this was denied. Sex was only supposed to exist for the purpose of begetting children. Now, of course, in our generation it is necessary to say that this is one of the purposes of marriage, because too many young people today don't even want to bother with the burden of children. So we emphasize that this is a duty. God says we are to be fruitful and multiply. Yet, at the same time, it is equally important to stress what is clearly taught in this part of the Scripture. And it teaches us that sexual love has its own value. It's wrong to treat this as though it were some evil. When God gives us a beautiful book like this in the Bible, you can see that this can't be right. And when God himself likens this sexual love between husband and wife to the love of Christ for the church, you can see that this can't be right. And it isn't right, and it's done a lot of harm in the church to suppress this. Part of the problem today in our society and culture is the boomerang effect from that wrong denial and suppression of biblical truth. When the wedding between Christ and his bride comes, there isn't going to be any purpose to multiply at all. The multiplication will all be ended, and the one and only thing that will exist in that eternal marriage between Christ and the church is their taking delight in each other. That never should have been suppressed.

And then, finally, I want to emphasize again *the comfort and assurance that we have in this part of God's Word.* The Song of Solomon, the Song of Songs, is not for those who have a perfect track record. This book wasn't just written for those who never made a misstep. Not at all. Christ's bride was a no-good to start with. You know that because you're part of the bride of Christ, and you're no good by nature, but God has redeemed you. He's given you a new heart, and a new nature. And that's why you find people like Rahab the harlot mentioned in the Bible, who became an ancestor of Jesus. And that's why you also find what Paul teaches in Ephesians 5 in that matter of fact passage when he discusses husband and wife, and their duty to each other, and then suddenly says, "This is a profound mystery—but I am talking about Christ and the church" (Eph. 5:32). The reason he speaks of Christ and the church, when he is talking about earthly husbands and wives, is that in the ultimate sense you can't speak of one without the other. You can't really talk about God's standard of marriage for us without talking about Christ and the church. And you can't talk about Christ and the church without setting before God's people the model of marriage.

You know sometimes people have said to me, "Why do I need all this doctrine? Why do I need to worry about the doctrine of the church, and of Christ, and sin?" Well, my dear friends, you can't even begin to have a foundation for marriage until you know these great doctrines, do you know that? It's a fact. The one depends upon the other, because the one is based upon the analogy of the other. And it's only when we understand these things, and enter into the ordinances of God, and think and live his way that he pronounces his benediction and says, "Now, enjoy yourself to the full. Eat and drink, O lovers," and that really is lovers' liberation.

Amen.

5

The Test of True Love, Part 1

Song of Solomon 5:2–6:9

Over these past few weeks, congregation, we have been thinking of this great and ideal marriage, and the things that led up to it—how they met, the progress of their courtship, and, at last, the actual wedding ceremony itself and the consummation of their love. And I've pointed out to you several times that there is a very good reason why God chose this form of revelation. I suppose it would have been unthinkable for a poem to have been written at that time that was critical of the king, and so all the problems in this song are in the wife and not the husband. That's not the way it is, for us, in everyday life as you all know—especially you who are women. You have problems with the men just as much as we have problems with the women (and, again, we remember that in this world there is no such a thing as a perfect marriage). I used to imagine that there could be, when I was really young, but when I grew up and had one of my own—and then ministered to other people—I soon learned that it is impossible. You can't take a daughter of Eve and marry her to a son of Adam and have a perfect marriage—it's not possible.

Yet in this particular marriage, what you have is Solomon set forth as the ideal husband, and the problems are found in his wife, the Shulamite. And this, I think, is for a very good reason in God's providential purpose. It's because standing behind this marriage of Solomon and the Shulamite is the greater model of the love of Christ for the church. And I'm sure you'll agree that in the love between Christ and the church all the problems are on the wife's side. There is no fault in Jesus. He is absolutely perfect—100 percent sinless. But the church is far from perfect. She's not yet sanctified completely. Again and again she has been unfaithful to *her* husband, Christ Jesus. And so in the very way in which this song was written we are constantly reminded of that higher and ultimate model of the one perfect marriage—the marriage between Christ and his church.

We begin, then, by taking note of the fact that in this marriage of Solomon and the Shulamite there arose something of a *crisis*. You can see that when she says, "I slept but my heart was awake" (5:2). She had a dream, but she was also keenly aware in her dream, and she was thinking about things in their relationship, the one with the other.

Now the Bible says that dreams arise out of the multitudes of life's vexations (Eccles. 5:3). If you have dreams very often, and analyze them, they will often tell you something about yourself. When I was a young minister, I used to dream again and again about being late for the worship service. I would rush around looking for my shoes and couldn't find them. I would hear the congregation starting to sing and frantically rush to get there. Next week I would dream the same dream again, only this time I couldn't find my sermon notes and was absolutely frantic. Then, just at the last moment, as the hymn was about to end, I would find them and then run for the church. And then the dream ended, and I never found out what happened. The dream happened over and over again, and it wouldn't take somebody like Sigmund Freud to tell you my problem was anxiety; I didn't feel confident enough, I didn't feel well prepared enough. You see, dreams arise out of the vexations of life.

Well, this woman also had a dream, and in it there was a kind of replay of one of the problems that was vexing their marriage. So what was the problem? The problem was this. She heard her lover knocking at the door, and he said, "Open to me, my sister, my darling, my dove" (5:2). My goodness, he uses plenty of loving terms, doesn't he? But what does she say in reply? She says, "I have taken off my robe—must I put it on again? I have washed my feet—must I soil them again?" (5:2). In other words, "Really, do you have to put me to all this trouble?" That's what she really was saying. And that is a common thing in marriage—a growing reluctance to put yourself out for the other person. I've noticed that when two young people come to arrange to get married, they usually knock themselves out to please each other. "What do you want, honey?" "Oh, I don't know. What do you want?" "Whatever you say." "No, whatever you say." And so it goes back and forth between them. They bend over backward to accommodate each other. But here, a few months, maybe a few years later, she says, "Do I have to get up and get my feet soiled for you, honey?" This is true to human nature and human experience.

Now, the problem isn't that she doesn't love him anymore; that's quite clear. If she didn't love him anymore, she wouldn't have such a dream. She wouldn't be anxious about it. She wouldn't get up with her heart pounding and go looking for him through the town—almost a replay of that dream she had before they were married, only this time things are a lot worse than they were then. This time they start to beat her. Yes, that's what it says. "The watchmen found me," and what did they do? "They beat me, they bruised me; they took away my cloak, those watchmen of the walls!" (5:7). They didn't do that earlier when she was anxious about whether she would get this guy tied down in the first place, but now, you see, she is really anxious about their relationship, and that proves to you that she really loves him. And the way she speaks about him shows that, and the way she goes out looking desperately for him, and says, "O daughters of Jerusalem . . . if you find [him]. . . . Tell him I am faint with love" (5:8).

Our text doesn't tell us exactly what had caused the problem. She's having a dream, and she's revealing this problem that has probably had a lot of different types of manifestation in their lives. And again I think we'll have to compare this to the little foxes that we met when they were in courtship. You remember how the little foxes were there. And Solomon in his wisdom said, "You've got to get the little foxes out of the vineyard." And we interpreted and explained that to mean that you've got to learn to handle the little problems before they get too big. That's one of the purposes of courtship, and if you can't handle it in courtship, look out, because marriage is going to be even harder.

Well, this problem here is not a big elephant—not yet. It's still like one of these little foxes. And I would say it probably came out of a scenario like this. You get married, and you get into the humdrum existence of life—you have a few children, you have a house to look after—and you begin to become vexed by the burden of daily cares and concerns. Now that's natural. We all have an experience like that. One of my friends who was a professor at Westminster was having breakfast one day when he let his daughter run around under his feet, and accidentally she pulled on the electric cord and down came the hot coffee pot and spilled boiling coffee on her. And they had to drop everything and rush to the hospital, and for two or three days they were there at her side, not another thought in their mind but the way it would turn out for that little girl. Now that's natural, that's right, that's good, but there is such a thing as to let the routine duties of life crowd out what should always be number one in any marriage and that is the concern that the husband has for his wife and the wife has for her husband.

And here again the analogy is very clear because you know what happens when the church lets something else crowd out the one thing that ought to always be central. And that is the fervency of its devotion to the Lord Jesus. One of the things that has been happening in some Reformed churches across the world in our generation is something we call a move from the vertical to the horizontal—less concern about God Almighty and his worship and faithfulness to him, and more concern about social and political problems. Now, of course, we should be concerned about social and political problems. We all ought to have some concern about such things as AIDS and abortion. But when the church becomes preoccupied with anything horizontal, and it loses the fervency of its devotion and love for Christ (the vertical) as number one, then you're going to have all kinds of problems.

Do you remember the woman who came and anointed Jesus's feet and wept and wiped them with her hair? The disciples were horizontalists in their thinking. They said, "What a stupid, ridiculous thing. That could have been sold for a lot of money. And we could have taken that money, and we could have helped a lot of poor people." But Jesus said, "Let her alone. She has done the right thing. She has things in the right order. She has anointed me for my burial, and I'm more important than those people who are starving." And that's a fact, and if we ever forget that in the church, look out, because the same thing happens in our relationship with Christ that happened here between this woman and her husband. She let something else become more important—for the time being—than her husband, and that is not right. And when you do that, like it or not, other things tend to go wrong also.

I think that's the significance in the dream of the watchmen beating her. If you're married and things aren't right between you and your wife—or you and your husband—isn't it true that everything else seems lousy also? You get mad at the world. You feel like kicking the toaster across the kitchen. Everything else is out of order in the home when things are not right between a wife and her husband. That is the significance of her dream. She let other things come first. She couldn't be bothered. And now she realizes that life itself has become miserable, and everything else is lousy, too. Well, that's psychologically true.

The second thing we deal with, then, is *Solomon's answer to this problem.* For what does he do? Well, what do you do? Do you retaliate? I think that's what we all tend to do, because of our sinful nature. "If she's not going to do that for me; I'm not going to do it for her either. Just wait till the next time that she asks me for something—because I'm not going to forget this." Sometimes a husband responds that way, giving her a little of her own medicine (to put it bluntly). And Solomon could have said to her, "Listen, I'm the head of the house, and you'd better acknowledge it." He can come down with a heavy foot, in other words—that's another way that you can handle the situation, and I've known husbands to do it. I've even seen a third reaction. He can give her the silent treatment. He can simply pout and say nothing. But Solomon didn't do any of these. When she couldn't be bothered to get up and soil her feet, do you know what he did? He went off and got busy with other tasks that he had to do. That's why she couldn't find him.

Now, of course, this is in her dream, but this was also characteristic of him—instead of retaliating, he got busy and involved in some other job and got it done. I think that has to be true, because otherwise in her dream there would have been some reflection of retaliation and there isn't the slightest bit of this. It's not for nothing that Solomon is called the wisest man in the Bible prior to our Lord Jesus. So *he* knew what a lot of husbands aren't wise enough to know—he knew that retaliation only aggravates the problem. I found that out the hard way a few times, and I suppose that many of you have. It only makes matters worse. So he simply went out and got busy with other things. One commentator even suggests that he left a little perfume on the handle of the door. I don't know if that's a little fanciful. When she went to the door, it says her hands dripped with myrrh and her fingers with flowing myrrh, so maybe that's true, but anyway it is perfectly evident that he did not respond in kind but acted in love. And one act of love will do more good than a hundred acts of retaliation. If you really want to get to that wife of yours, or that husband of yours, when he or she has been lousy, do something nice. That is the "coup de grace," as they say, because that is the power of love, and doesn't that bring us right back to the way it was in the beginning?

What was it that won her heart to this man in the first place? Do you remember when she said, "His banner over me is love"? Do you remember how we traced that out in the Bible? When you go into battle, you have a banner. You don't want to go into battle and meet the enemy and risk death, but because of that banner you'll go. Because of your patriotic feeling, you'll go. Well, she says, his banner over me is love. Not force, not unkindness, not being tough—but love. That's what made me willing to submit and sit under his shadow. And now here it is all over again, and she says, "What a wonderful man he is." And she saw that everything else in their marriage really rested upon the nobility of his love. I think that's why there is a parallel between this dream and the earlier one. Do you remember how she went out to look for her husband-to-be? Do you remember how she couldn't find him? They tried to help her, but now they don't help her, and she realizes in that very thing that all is lost if she doesn't have his love.

And right here is the parallel between Christ and the church. When anything goes wrong with our devotion to Jesus, everything else goes wrong, too. Do you know that when liberal churches deny the doctrines of grace and no longer preach faithfully the whole counsel of God found in the Bible, mission work also begins to wither and die, the sense of the church's mission in the world begins to fade out? Some people in the history of the church woke up to that fact, and thought, "Where is God? Where is our relationship to Christ?" And then you have a reformation, and the church goes back to fervent devotion to the Lord. That's what happened in the Reformation. The people again filled the churches, and poured out their hearts to the living God in fervent worship, and then God poured out his blessing and everything began to go right again.

That's exactly what you have here in this chapter. For the first time, in this context, she describes his beauty. Twice already he has described her beauty, but now for the first time she describes *his* beauty. I reckon that's about par for the course. Women are far more beautiful than we men are—everybody knows that. It's only natural that she should be described several times before he is, but now he is described. You see it starting in 5:10. She talks about how radiant he is.

His head is purest gold, his eyes are like doves, his cheeks are like beds of fragrance, and so on. She really does think he's attractive, and it's really because he's so wonderful in his love. I don't think he's gotten any more handsome. I think it's just that his love has really got to her far more than ever before in their relationship. And that is the beauty of the way that it also is in our relationship with Christ. The Bible says we love him because he first loved us, and the deeper your awareness of the love of Christ—what he did for you—the more out of your heart will flow praise and adoration. And you also will say, he is the fairest among ten thousand, the one who is altogether lovely. It is his love that brings that response from the church.

We come, then, in the third place to *a beautiful reconciliation*, and here I would like to stress once again the covenant aspect of marriage. In 6:1, we again have one of these rhetorical questions, and to my mind it doesn't really matter who asks it—the daughters of Jerusalem? Solomon himself in a kind of rhetorical aside? Because it ultimately is Almighty God himself who asks this question: "Where has your lover gone, most beautiful of women? Which way did your lover turn, that we may look for him with you?" (6:1). And she says, "My lover has gone down to his garden" (6:2).

If you were to put that question to many of the young people in our land today (both in and not in marriage under vows) they would have no answer. "Where is he?" they would say. "I don't know; I wish I did know"—that's what many of them would have to say. "I don't have any strings on that guy." And a lot of guys would say, "I don't know where she is. I don't have any strings on her." There are many so-called open marriages today. And a lot of churches have watered down the vows of marriage until they really don't mean much. The result is that you're not bound to anything. If you want to walk in, you can walk in. And if you want to walk out, you can walk out.

But covenantal marriage, as God ordained it, is entirely different. You can't walk out. No, you promised for better or worse, for richer or poorer, in sorrow as well as in happiness, that you will not forsake her or him as long as you both will live. And where you have covenantal marriage, there is security, and you *know* where that other person is. They might be upset, they might be a little bit angry, but you *know* where they are. And you know where you can find them, because you know you can depend on them. So she says, "I know where he is." And in 6:3 she tells us why she knows, for she says, "I am my lover's and my lover is mine." And you can only say *that* in the context of covenantal, Christian marriage—"she is mine, and I am hers." And there are no ifs, and no ands, and no buts. That's the way it really is, and that's the way God intended it to be—in spite of the trials and problems.

And here again the great model is Christ and the church. For one of the things we *know* as God's covenantal people (and how wonderful it is to know it) is that in spite of all our failures and imperfections, he has promised, "I will never leave you, I will never forsake you." Christ Jesus came down here to this world to save his church. On the night on which he was betrayed, he gathered with them for the last supper. They were arguing about who would be top man under him in the kingdom; they were bickering and fighting. And the Bible says, "Having loved His own who were in the world, He loved them to the end" (John 13:1 NJKV). That's why he took the towel and began to wash their feet. But the point I make is that his love never wavered.

So, she comes down there looking for him, and what does he say to her? "Well, it's about time you got here?" No, he doesn't. He's too smart, too wise for that. Some of us probably would say that, but not Solomon, a type of the Lord Jesus. What does he say? He says right away, with the first words out of his mouth, "You are beautiful, my darling. . . . Turn your eyes from me; they overwhelm me" (6:4–5). And then he begins, again, to praise the beauty of this woman.

Now, I think you would agree as you read that passage that it is far less sensual, far less sexual in its overtone than was the earlier description. And there is a very good reason. Right now is psychologically the perfect time to tell her that he values her for what she *is*, not just what he can get out of her. You know, the Greeks had different words for love. They had the word *eros*, from which we get our word *erotic*. They had *phileo* for friendship love, the kind of love that binds two people together who really like one another. But they also had another word that they didn't use very much—and that's exactly why the New Testament chose that word and filled it full of a great content. It is the great word *agape*, the kind of love that is steadfast and immovable, the kind of love that doesn't depend on some loveliness in the object loved, but on the steadfast character of the one who does the loving. And it was the agape love, the faithful love of Christ for his church, that again and again has won the church's heart to him. And it was the love of this wise Solomon that kindled in the Shulamite—more than ever—her love in response to her husband.

So here again you see the ultimate model—the absolutely faithful covenant love that conquers our hearts completely. For what is it that conquers our hearts to Christ in real commitment? Is it is his awesome *authority*—the fact that he has all authority in heaven and earth—is that why you're committed to Jesus? Is it because of your *fear* of his terrible wrath? Is it because you respect his almighty *power* that you are committed to Jesus? No, of course not—it's because of his love, the fact that he loved us and gave himself for us that he might cleanse us and that we might stand before him holy and without blame; and because he never gives up on us, even though we are so unworthy. You know, when we realize this, this love of Christ for the church, beautifully set forth as in a model in Solomon and his bride, and by the grace of God begin to enter into it, we begin to have the key to a beautiful marriage.

I began by saying there is no such thing as a perfect marriage, and that's true. But it's also true that in the church of Christ there are such things as beautiful marriages. God's people do grow up in all things into Jesus. And it is possible for people today—the more they understand what Christ is to the church and what the church is to Christ—to begin to manifest that same love in a beautiful way in marriage, home, and family. One of the greatest needs in the church today is to see that in Christian marriages and families. What a wonderful witness whenever the world sees an image of Christ's love for his church, and the church's love for Christ in the lives of his people. And the wonderful thing is that you, by the grace of God, can have a part in that witness.

May God grant it, for Christ's sake.

Amen.

6

The Test of True Love, Part 2

Song of Solomon 6:10–8:4

Congregation, I want to remind you once again that the Song of Solomon is a one-sided presentation of Christian marriage. In the time that this book was written, it was not a thing of propriety to say anything bad about the king, and so all the faults in the book that we are looking at here are in the bride rather than in the bridegroom—in the Shulamite rather than in Solomon—and that is certainly not true in one of our marriages. But we can be thankful that the providence of God brought this about because God wanted this book to be a reflection of the ultimate model, the marriage between Christ and the church.

We have followed these two young people as they met, as they conducted their courtship, as they had a joyful marriage ceremony and a consummation in love together, and then the last time we met we saw how problems and difficulties arose. And when those problems and difficulties arose, you'll remember how the Shulamite had a bad dream, reflecting the anxious fears that she felt she might somehow lose him. And

71

not only that but other things began to go wrong, too, until she desired to get things right again, and she went out looking for him, forgetting herself; and she knew where to go because their marriage was a covenant relationship. And you remember how when she did go down to where Solomon was, he didn't retaliate against her; he didn't reply in kind; he acted in love. And she instantly knew all over again that his banner over her was indeed love. And right away the flowers began to bloom, and the birds began to sing. There love was better than ever. And she knew more than ever before how much she loved him. That's where we are in the context of this book, and tonight we look at the root of this crisis which, I believe, really comes in every Christian marriage. Then, after we have traced the root of the crisis, I want you to see what tremendous blessings come when that crisis is resolved in the way of God's ordaining.

Now, what was the ultimate cause, the root of the crisis that came in the marriage of Solomon and the Shulamite maiden? Well, of course, it traces back to what happened to our first parents. The Bible says that when our first parents sinned against God, they immediately fell into a state of corruption. They were not only driven out of a wonderful *place*, but they also fell from of a wonderful *state* of perfection. You can see that because right away this great and terrible process of blame-shifting began in their relationship with each other. And you remember that God pronounced that terrible judgment, and you can read what he said to the woman in Genesis 3:16, which I believe is one of the most frequently misunderstood texts in the Bible. The Lord God said to the woman, "Your desire will be for your husband." Right through the history of the church, that has almost always been taken to mean that she would desire—would have a love relationship toward her husband that would triumph over everything—yes, even the fear of the pain of childbearing. You remember that in that same context the Lord said that in pain she will bring forth children, and the idea has been in the common interpretation that the Lord is saying, "Even though that is true—there will be pain—your desire will triumph over that for your desire will be for your husband."

Well, I'm indebted to a woman for putting me right on this one. Her name is Susan Foh. She's wrote a very fine book on the role of woman. And she is a very fine Hebraist. She is the one who pointed out to me, at least, the almost amazing similarity of Genesis 3:16, Genesis 4:7, and part of our text for tonight. In Genesis 4:7, you'll notice that the Lord God had something to say to Cain after he sinned. The Bible says the Lord came to Cain and said, "Why are you angry? Why is your face downcast? If you do what is right, will you not be accepted? But if you do not do what is right, sin is crouching at your door; it desires to have you, but you must master it" (Gen. 4:6–7). Now, that phrase, "It desires to have you," is exactly the same kind of Hebrew expression that you have in what God said to Cain. And what is the relationship between sin, crouching at the door, and Cain? Well, it's clearly an antagonistic relationship, isn't it? The Lord is urging Cain to do the right thing—to follow the pattern and example of his brother. But he also recognizes that sin, which is crouching at the door, desires to have the mastery over Cain. As a matter of fact, sad to say, that's the way it turned out. What Susan Foh says—and I think she is quite right—is that what's really being said in Genesis 3:16 is that, as a result of the fall, there is a kind of an adversarial relationship between the woman and her husband. Her desire is against her husband, and what that really means is this: sin did something to the human race, and one of the things it did was to create in a woman's heart a rebellious attitude toward her role assignment. She doesn't want to be under the authority of her husband. There is something in the heart of every woman, as a daughter of Eve, which inclines her to some degree to resist the lawful headship of her husband.

Let me put it this way: you women don't really want to be ruled by your husbands by nature. You don't. That's a fact, and that's why many of you men smiled as soon as I said that. You know it's true. Now, I realize that in saying that, I've only given a part of the picture, because the Bible also says that we husbands ought to love our wives as Christ loved the church. And you have every right to say, "There sure is something wrong with you fellows, too, because you don't do what you should either. You don't come within a hundred miles of doing it." And I agree; we don't. And that's because of what sin has done to our fallen nature.

The fact remains, however, and this is the point of our text, the problem that arose between the Shulamite and her husband really grew out of this sinful tendency by which the wife doesn't want to be subject all the time to her husband. That's why, in this book, the problem is in the wife; because, of course, in the great model, the ultimate model—which is the love of Christ for the church and his marriage with his bride, the church—Christ does love with a perfect love, and it is the church which often puts her own will in opposition to the will of her husband. That is really what brought about this crisis, and whether it is from the wife's side or the husband's side or from both sides, it is always the root of the crisis.

There wouldn't be any crisis in your marriage or mine, if the man *always* loved his wife as Christ loved the church, *and* the woman was *always* willing to be under the loving leadership of her husband, with all her heart, with all her soul, with all her mind, and with all her strength. There wouldn't be this problem in marriage arising from this root cause that traces back to the fall of man. But now in the rest of this section we are going to see what happens when this wife recognizes that she's been acting sinfully (as we saw she did recognize last time) and stops thinking about her own will and desire and begins to think about her husband. She wants things to be right again, and so she now forgets herself and goes out until she finds him, and they experience togetherness and love again. And we'll see the blessings that come to her when she once again is willing to be under the loving leadership of her husband.

And just look at what happened. The first thing you see— and this is really remarkable—is that her status is immediately lifted higher than ever. Now I suppose that at the root of the resistance in the female heart to the headship of the man is a desire for status, isn't it? And yet what happens when she really does submit to her role assignment the way God wants her to? Why, right away she is exalted. She goes up and not down. "Who is this that appears like the dawn [the first rays of light], fair as the moon [that's more light], bright as the sun [that's more light], majestic as the stars [you've got all of it there]?" (6:10). And somehow the writers know that the stars were greater in magnitude than the sun, and they are. So what you have here, emblematically presented, is the wonder and beauty and the rising glory of this wife because she has again put herself willingly under the headship of her husband. And that's a beautiful thing to see.

I think all you women would agree that if you were to make a survey of the Bible and ask who are really the great women and what really made them great women, this would be the thing. There's hardly any exception to that rule. I don't believe there is any exception. The higher a woman's reputation and luster in the Bible, the clearer it is that she evidenced this submission. Think of Deborah, and how she respected the headship of the man. She had to prop up Barak to get him to do his duty, and the result is that she got the glory. And you remember Abigail, the wife of Nabal "the fool," and what a fool he was, but she got the glory because she did not try to bring him down; she let him do that for himself. And she was honored. She was a true mother of Israel.

So here we read that this woman goes down to the grove of nut trees. And what happens? "Before I realized it," she said—she wasn't even thinking of status, you see—"my desire"—that's Solomon—"set me among the royal chariots of my people" (6:12). She was right up there on the throne beside him again. Her status was exalted. And I believe that this will happen in the life of any woman who's willing to live God's way. As sure as you from the heart say, "I know I'm not married to the perfect husband, but I know what my Lord wants me to do, and I'm going to do it for his glory. I'm going to willingly submit to the leadership of my husband." Well, that woman's status begins to go up right there and then, as sure as I'm standing here; that's a fact. If you exalt yourself, the Bible says you're going to be humbled. And exalting yourself is exactly what you are doing if you don't like the role that God gives you, and then try to work out something better—what you're trying to do is exalt yourself. And you're going to be humbled, you're going to go down. But the Bible says, "Humble yourselves under the mighty hand of God, that He may exalt you" (1 Peter 5:6 NKJV). Now the Lord did that for Abigail even though she was married to a fool. He was rightly named "Mr. Fool," because that's what he was. But God exalted her, and through her wisdom brought her to be a wife of King David.

Isn't that exactly the picture we get in the book of Proverbs? I hope you're all familiar with that beautiful passage we get in the last chapter of the book of Proverbs where the woman, the ideal woman, you might say, is pictured. And she rejoices in the role of her husband—he is an elder at the gate, and she is supporting him. She is building him up. She is doing everything she can to promote her husband's honor in the land of Israel. And what happens? Does her status go down? Not on your life; it goes up. And the scope of her activities—is it shrinking? Not on your life; it's expanding. If you humble yourself under the mighty hand of God, and you say, "Lord God, I now by your grace have a willing heart and I want to do what you have given me to do," right then and there your status goes up. Not only that but (and I would suppose that this would also be important to any woman) she immediately becomes more beautiful.

"Come back, come back, O Shulamite, Come back, come back that we may gaze on you." I don't know who says that, but I suppose it was most likely a whole bunch of people there in the nation of Israel. They've noticed that there's something different about her. Her husband also immediately thinks she's more beautiful than ever.

Now, you remember that when this Solomon married her, he already praised her beauty in what we might call hard-to-top terms. He described her physical beauty in a sevenfold poem of praise, and I told you at the time that in the Hebrew culture if you wanted to tell a woman that she was practically perfect, you would use seven to do it. Well, now, how are you going to top seven? If you were part of the Hebrew culture, you would immediately know the answer. There's only one way, and that is to mention ten things instead of seven. And if you can do it in a poem describing ten beautiful features in that woman, then you've topped it. And that's what he does here. You can go right through chapter 7, and you can count them—there are ten of her physical features that he praises and extols. That's his way of telling her that she is more beautiful by far, than when they first started out. And that must make any woman realize how fortunate she is to have a husband like that. And that's exactly why—when you submit under God's ordinances—his blessings are so evident.

I should also point out the fact that this is probably the most sensual and sexual of all the descriptions of love in the entire Bible, and it's what you might call the second plateau of marriage. I think this illustrates again how wrong the church has been in not being willing to speak frankly about these matters, but let me emphasize the fact that you always have to see these matters in the proper context. The modern approach to sex is in terms of its mechanics. You've got to know all the facts. That's the really sinister threat about bringing sex education into the schools, because if you just know all the mechanical facts, you don't really know what you need to know. As you can plainly see, the problem in this marriage wasn't that they didn't know the facts, that they didn't know about the biology of the human body. It had nothing whatsoever to do with that; they knew that all right. The problem was that for a while they weren't on God's wavelength in their fundamental obedience to his will. When that was straightened out, sex was no problem. And that's what you'll never have out of a Christian context. You won't have it. And that's why sex education in a secular school is terribly harmful, not helpful. It's harmful because the foundation of life—the whole thing—is covenantal; you've got to be right with God. You've got to have a willing heart to live by his ordinances. Then, these other things will begin to assume their proper place. Seek first the kingdom of God and his righteousness, and then all these other things will be added unto you. You see, that's the principle here.

And a third thing that you see in this passage is this—and I think it's wonderful, and every woman is really missing out if she doesn't see it— for *immediately this woman found a new freedom*; so much so that the words of the curse are completely inverted. She says, "May the wine go straight to my lover, flowing gently over lips and teeth. I belong to my lover, and his desire is *for* me" (7:9–10). Now those are identically the words that you have in Genesis 3:16 and 4:7 with one little change, one little Hebrew letter is changed, and that makes all of the difference. The difference is that there is no longer an *antagonism*, but rather the desire of *promotion*. "His desire is not *against* me," she says, "no, it is for me." And right away you begin to see it in their relationship because under his loving leadership, she has far greater scope for her own initiative. She's the one who says, "Come, my lover, let us go to the countryside" (7:11). In other words, she takes an initiative quite freely within the context of a willing submission to his leadership, and he gladly allows it. If you have a heart that's really willing to submit God's ordinances, that doesn't diminish your freedom. To the contrary it enlarges and opens it up. It becomes greater.

Did you ever notice that in a good marriage you see both of these aspects together? I've seen people who have been married and happy in their marriage where the man calls his wife *darling*, and then a few minutes later he'll speak of her as *mother*. I used to think that was a little bit funny, but the longer I live the more I see that is perfectly right and biblical. It's an added dimension to the marriage, and you see that in our text. "If only you were to me like a brother," she says. ". . . Then, if I found you outside, I would kiss you, and no one would despise me" (8:1). She would have a kind of right, in other words, in a playful way to mother him. Well, that becomes also a perfectly proper dimension of the loving relationship within God's covenant, and it's also due to the fact that he has learned to appreciate her counsel and wisdom.

And when she's no threat to his leadership, all the more does he want that and seek it and promote it. She is given more and more freedom. The woman in Proverbs 31, who really has her heart set in the ways of God and heartily submits to her husband's leadership, can hardly take any more than the responsibility he gives her. So, you see, God's way never diminishes anybody; it always enlarges the scope of their potential.

And here, again, you can see so clearly the ultimate model in the love of Christ and the church. For, if you know anything about the Reformed faith, you will know this has been the glory of the Reformed faith. Christ alone is King and Head of the church. The Bible alone is the infallible rule of our faith and practice. We don't want human inventions cluttering up the worship of God; we want the simplicity and purity of doing what our Savior commands. And what happens when the church really lives in that? It's exalted, and you see this so clearly in the Reformation. But what happens to the church when it begins to set its will in opposition to Christ's headship and says, "No, not the Bible alone? We're not going to be restricted to what God says; we're going to do our own thing"? What happens to the church then? Well, its glory fades away, and its status is diminished. And it is not respected by anyone—especially not by the world. But what happens when the church *is* revived, and is willing to submit once more to the sovereign authority of Christ and the absolute inerrancy of the Bible? Is its freedom diminished? Not on your life. That's when the church really is free. You really stand tall and free in the world when you stand as a church on that firm basis.

I hope that this is what we will more and more see in our own generation—churches that really do submit to the authority of Christ as it is revealed in the Bible. That is the true glory of the church, and that is its real freedom. We are, of all the people in the land, free if we really have that. If we lose it, we haven't got freedom any more. I used to get a paper in the mail—I didn't subscribe to it—I think it was called *Innovations* and that is certainly what it was filled with. It just revealed to me how sick many churches are today, because it was full of gimmicks, invented by preachers all over the land, to try to keep a dead body looking as if it's still living. Do all sorts of clever, gimmicky things to stir up the people and keep them interested. It reminded me of an entertainer who has to try to think up new jokes every week, to keep people laughing. It's like that in many churches. And when I read that paper I said to myself, "How sad that they have lost it." We don't need gimmicks—we only need to know that we are really doing what God says to do in his Word. If we are really doing that, you can depend on it—he's going to exalt us. That's what he will do. And he will make us conscious of the glory of our freedom.

And now you notice that we come once again, for the last time, to this remarkable statement that we've already met twice before: "Daughters of Jerusalem, I charge you: Do not arouse or awaken love until it so desires" (8:4). Do you remember why and when she said that before? She said it before they ever got married. And she said it because she did not want to enter into the sanctuary of love until it was pleasing to God. She wanted to wait until God's approval was given and then give herself to that man completely. Here you see there's something in that principle that applies to all life, as it applies in courtship. It's really like saying, "I've already learned in life that the golden rule of marriage is to stay within the guidelines of holy Scripture. If you do that you're going to be blessed. If you depart from it, you're going lose it." That's what we clearly see here in this life of this married couple.

What you have, in other words, in Christian marriage—modeled after the love of Christ for the church—is a foretaste of paradise. Adam and Eve had it once, but then they lost it. God said to her, "Your desire is going to be *against* your husband." But here—in the Song of Songs—we see the wonderful fact that where the grace of God is operative in the hearts of two covenant-keeping people that curse is greatly diminished. To a greater and greater degree for those who love the Lord and are willing to walk in his ways, it is turned around, and paradise is regained. That's what Christian marriage can be. And don't you think, too, that that's what the world needs to see today—in this day when marriage, home, and family are crumbling at a frightening rate?

I hope you realize that even as we meet here the foundations are crumbling all over the land because of the breakdown of marriage. And our nation isn't going to be strong ten, twenty, fifty years down the road if this trend continues—because the strength of a nation rests on the strength of its families. And that strength has always been found primarily in God's covenant people. If you are willing to live God's way, you're going to have that strength and beauty. That's the central point truth taught in this book. And it's a wonderful thing to know that even in the midst of a degenerate time like this God can still do wonders. And you can have it today as surely as at any other time because it's a matter of heart-willingness to live the way God wants us to live. "You will know the truth," said Jesus, "and the truth will set you free" (John 8:32). And when it sets you free as it did the Shulamite girl, then everything begins to be lovely and begins to bring honor to Jesus. May our prayer be that he will enable us to show forth his glory in the same way.

Amen.

7

The Love That Excels

Song of Solomon 8:5-8:7

Congregation of the Lord Jesus, I want to begin this sermon by talking, first of all, about the language of the Bible and the levels of love that it reveals. The Greek language was a highly inflected and discriminating language. And they had at least three different words for love, while we only have one to cover the various meanings. So when they came to translate the Old Testament into the Greek language, the language of the nations, they used these three different terms in a discriminating way.

One of the most common words for love in the Greek language is the Greek word *eros*. It's the word from which we, today, get our English word *erotic*. It is a word that functions on the level of the sensual, the bodily, and the sexual. We find it at least once in the Greek Bible in Proverbs 7. Here Solomon describes a prostitute as she seeks to entice and allure a young man of the nation of Israel into a momentary sexual relationship with her. And she says, "I have perfumed my bed with myrrh, aloes and cinnamon. Come, let's drink deep of love till morning; let's enjoy ourselves with love!" (Prov. 7:17–18). Well, in the context it's quite obvious the word *eros* (translated as *love* in English) means nothing more here than biological, sexual excitement.

Now, we've already seen, as we've gone through this book, that *eros* is a legitimate part of marriage. We saw that quite clearly in the early chapters of the Song of Solomon, where the elements of physical attraction, sensuality, and beauty were perfectly normal and recognized as such by the people of God. Biblical Christianity doesn't deny that and doesn't want to deny that; it doesn't want to pretend that we are super-spiritual mystics like they did in the Middle Ages, as if the body were really the source of all evil. It's not that at all. The heart is the thing out of which come the issues of life. And so the Bible is very frank in acknowledging the proper role and place of the erotic. That's why in this Song of Solomon, the Shulamite maiden expressed a great care and reserve so she didn't separate this aspect of marriage from the other aspects. She didn't want anyone to arouse love on that level before the right time had come.

The second level of love in Scripture is found in the Greek word *phileo*, from which we get words like *Philadelphia*, the city of brotherly love, or *philosopher*, the person who loves wisdom. And you already have that right here in this book in 5:16 when she says, concerning Solomon, "This is my lover, this my friend." She's talking there about love on the *phileo* level, where there is the love of companionship and enjoyment of each other—friendship as well as the purely erotic. And I believe every good marriage ought to have this in it. You know, we sometimes look at the world in which we live, and while there is much that distresses us, isn't it true that sometimes we are truly amazed at what appear to be stable and enduring marriages among people who are not Christian at all. They have no knowledge of—and devotion to—Christ the Savior, and yet they have a marriage that seems to be enduring and even enjoyable. What is the reason? I believe it is because they have built into that marriage much more than merely the erotic. They have also a love on the *phileo* level; they have a community of interest; they share things together. Maybe it's something like art or a mutual respect for music, but they do have a fellowship and a friendship, one with the other.

You know, sometimes people have misunderstood what David said about the love that existed between him and Jonathan. David said it was "surpassing the love of women" (2 Sam. 1:26 NKJV), and a lot of people have taken umbrage at that, but you see David was the victim of an impersonal love life. He had so many wives and concubines that he never really found that fellowship of love on the phileo level with any woman. He found that kind of love with Jonathan. Jonathan was a loyal friend all through the years, through all the pressures and the vicissitudes of life, and there was something in David that recognized that this was love on a higher level, and he paid tribute to that love when he said that. It's too bad that he missed that kind of love in fellowship with a wife. But, you see, he had too many of them. That's why you'll notice, in a good marriage, that there is a deepening of love reflected in their language. You notice in this Song that Solomon not only uses terms like *darling* and that sort of thing, but he calls her his sister, and she not only speaks of him in those words of sexual endearment but speaks of him as her friend and the like. This is something that can only come when we grow in the fellowship of companionship love, the love of *phileo*, and this ought to be a part of marriage in the Christian family.

There is, however, a higher word for love in the Bible, and it is reflected in the word *agape*, and the interesting thing is that the Greeks didn't use this word very often. It's found only a few times in the Greek writings. And I think that this is exactly why the New Testament writers—under the guidance of the holy Spirit, when they came along to write the story of the great love of God for man, as it is expressed in Jesus Christ—took this word that hadn't been used much and filled it with a new meaning. They filled it with the glorious content of the love of Jesus Christ, our Redeemer. So it became the word of the greatest importance in the New Testament Scriptures. The Greek word is *agape*, and it is only used of the love that excels. It is the love that does not depend, as the other two do, on something attractive in the other person. You can't command your daughter to sexually love another guy; it won't work. There has to be the spark of attraction there. She has to see some guy that somehow captures her desire. You can't command *phileo* love either. If you don't believe me, you try it. Say, "Son, I don't want you to be friends with John any more, I want you to be friends with Bill." I can tell you this: it's not going to work, because there has to be something in that other person that is attractive to draw out this *phileo* love as well. But the Bible *does* command *agape*. It does command the love that has as its sole motivating source something in the one who does the loving.

And we have seen that right here in the Song of Songs, in its highest expression, in the way Solomon dealt with his wife when she had been unloving, and unlovely. That was exactly when, instead of retaliating, instead of replying in kind, he showed her agape love. And I pointed out to you at the time that it had to be this way in the Song of Solomon. It had to be a one-sided story, with all the faults in the wife and all the virtues in the husband, because behind it stands the ultimate image of love, which is Christ and the church. There are no faults in Christ, and there are a lot of them in the church. And we—all of us, men and women alike—are the church, and we all have faults, but the point is that the love that excels is the love that not only has the erotic level and the companionship level but rises up even higher. It rises up to the level of the love that excels, the love patterned after the love of Christ for the church, the love patterned after Solomon for the Shulamite even when she wasn't lovely. It is the love that is described in the passage before us tonight. And this also ought to be in growing in every one of us and ought to be reflected in our marriages.

Now, what does this passage teach us about the love that excels? What is so special about it? I suggest first of all that *agape* love, the love at the highest level, is unique because of its willingness to endure pain and suffering.

> Who is this coming up from the wilderness,
> Leaning upon her beloved?
>
> I awakened you under the apple tree.
> There your mother brought you forth;
> There she who bore you brought you forth;
> Set me as a seal upon your heart. (8:5–6 NKJV)

Now, again, it doesn't make any difference who this speaker is in this rather rhetorical question in 8:5. God is the author, and he wants us to ask the question, What's so special about this? And then right away you'll notice the imagery of the tree. Now, maybe that tree again is the symbol of character. But maybe it's also a symbol, as it is in many cultures, of that place in the realm of nature where true love had its beginning. I can't say that I met my wife under the apple tree, but I can say that during World War II when I played in a big band, one of the popular love songs was exactly that. The apple tree in the song serves as a symbol of the place where these lovers met—where they fell in love, where they had a bit of romance. And I think that's really the idea that's right here in our text. That was the apple tree where it all began, he says.

But not only that, it's the apple tree—the same symbol— that involved your mother in labor, conception, and childbirth. In other words, it also involved pain; it involved the unpleasant; it involved self-denial and suffering. And in the biblical way of thinking, those who enter the realm of marriage accept that willingly as part of the purpose of God. You know one of the great tragedies in our civilization and society today is that so many people are rejecting this aspect of marriage. Fine, we'll have the erotic. Sure, we'll develop a fellowship and friendship sort of thing, but none of that childbearing for me. We're both going to be career people, and we're not going to get involved in any of that hassle. No, thank you. Or if we do, we're going to keep it to a very low minimum. Put them in an all-day care center, if possible. Get away from them as much as possible. Let somebody else suffer those tantrums and the weary work of bringing up those children. There's a lot of that today in our culture and society—an unwillingness to bear any pain or tribulation or suffering as a part of God's plan for sex and love and marriage. But it is part of God's plan—ask any father or mother who has raised children, and we all were children at one time, so we know that this is true. There are plenty of pains, plenty of sorrow and suffering. But the wonderful thing about love is that you don't regret it for one moment, not at all. It was in reality a joyful suffering in the deepest sense of the word, and that's what *agape* love is. You heard Paul describe it—it never gives up, never wears out, never gives out—because that love is like the love that God had for his people and Christ had for the church. And that is the love that excels, isn't it?

Now the second thing that we see about this love is that *it arises out of unshakable covenant commitment.*

> Place me like a seal over your heart,
>> like a seal on your arm;
> for love is as strong as death,
>> its jealousy unyielding as the grave.
> It burns like blazing fire,
>> like a mighty flame. (8:6)

In other words, it is covenanted love that rises up to the level where God is involved in the vows and commitment, in the way it ought to be in a good marriage. There's something unbreakable in this love. Sure, there is sorrow as well as joy, pain as well as pleasure, bad times as well as good, but you just don't think of giving up and walking out—that is *agape* love.

I think the greatest picture I ever saw of *agape* love was some years ago when I was serving in Kansas as a pastor in a little Reformed Presbyterian church there. What a tremendous exhibition of love. No, it wasn't two young people caught up in the tremendous heat and passion of eros. And it wasn't two people forty years of age really making it in the realm of *phileo.* No, it was two old people. I saw them in a rest home where we used to go to preach the gospel once a month, and every time I went there I saw this couple. It really wasn't a very pleasant sight, because you didn't have to look long to see that she'd had terrible stroke. She didn't even recognize the man beside her. And she said some unkind and hurtful things to him. Sometimes she would even suddenly slap him. And he was a distinguished, wonderful-looking old gentlemen. I didn't even have to ask if he was a Christian—I knew it from what I saw. He just talked to her gently and kept combing her hair and telling her what he'd been telling her for fifty years and more: "I love you, darling." That was the most beautiful exhibition of *agape* love I ever saw anywhere in this world. And that's the love that excels, the love that rests on covenant commitment. Now, I'm sure that this couple that I saw there in the rest home had once known the erotic. I'm sure they must have known the fellowship kind of love, too, but these were now gone. But *agape* love wasn't gone. I never saw it stronger than right there, and the pain that was there didn't destroy it at all. It only made it stronger.

And you know there's a book in the Bible about that. I don't know if you've ever read the book of Hosea with sharp-eyed attention to detail. Hosea married a woman, and he loved her and had three children by her. Gomer was her name. And then after a while, she decided she didn't like all the pain involved in being a mother, so she left home and went off and gave herself to one man and then another. At first she seemed to enjoy it, but then gradually she began to realize that it wasn't so wonderful just to be loved for the erotic and then left high and dry. There was no fellowship in it anywhere, nothing enduring. So, after a while she began to think, "I wish I was back with Hosea." Finally, she got up the nerve and went back to Hosea, a defiled image of her former beauty and glory.

What would you have done if you were Hosea? Would you open the front door and say, "Get lost"? Well, if the only thing you ever had with her was *eros*, that's exactly what you'd say. Who wants used merchandise like that? You might even say it if you'd never known anything better than companionship, because that's been down the tubes also, and for a long time. But if you ever had *agape* love—the love of covenant commitment—like the commitment we have from God in his holy and everlasting covenant of grace, like the love of Christ for the church, then you might understand Hosea. Because it was still there. It was there because many waters cannot quench *agape* love, nor will rivers overflow it. No, it wasn't destroyed, and so Hosea took her in again and loved her all over again and washed her filth away, just as Christ is washing his church with the water of the Word, bringing her out of the gutter of sin into the glorious presence of the love of God. That is the love that excels.

When you see that, you'll agree with the third thing I want to say about that love—the *incomparable value of it*, for many waters cannot quench love; rivers can't wash it away; if one were to give all the wealth of his house for *agape* love, it would be utterly scorned. In other words, the moment you try to put a price tag on the love that excels, you reduce it to absolute zero; you can't do that. You know, young people, you can buy erotic love in this world. One of the real shocks to me in coming back to the United States from overseas was the want-ads in some of the papers up and down the land in America. When I left this country, it wasn't true, but now in every daily paper in the big cities you have columns of sex for sale. It's legal now. No one does or says anything about it. For a few dollars, you can buy erotic love, and they say in some cultures you can buy companionship love too. I rather doubt that it was all that innocent, but I've heard it said that the purpose of the geisha in Japan was not *eros* but *phileo*. They were cultured and educated, and the wives weren't. They were good enough for erotic love, but for companionship love you went to the geisha. And you sat around drinking tea and talking about art and literature.

So, supposedly, you can even buy that—companionship—but you can never buy covenant love. It's not for sale, anywhere. The kind of love that Hosea had for Gomer. The kind of love that Solomon showed to the Shulamite after she'd been unkind to him, and he loved her anyway. The kind of love that Christ had for the church. You can't buy that love. So let me just ask you tonight, all of you that are married: Do you know love on the highest level? Of course you do if you're a Christian, because if you're a Christian you know that you're a sinner, that you've gone astray, and that you don't deserve the favor of Christ any more than the wife of Hosea did, for the Bible says, "We all, like sheep, have gone astray, each of us has turned to his own way" (Isa. 53:6). And what did Christ do? The Bible says, "Having loved His own who were in the world, He loved them to the end" (John 13:1 NJKV). He loved them to the uttermost. He did not cast them out. He did not give up on them. And so though our sins were as scarlet, he made them as white as wool, and he came and conquered our hearts, as fallen creatures, with his love—not with his wrath and judgment, but with his love. For you were not redeemed with corruptible things like silver and gold and precious stones—no, but by the precious blood of Jesus, which he shed that you might come back home and be his bride. And so he says to you, "Listen, you have been redeemed, you have been purchased, and *therefore* I expect you—when you go home to your husband or to your wife—to love them with that same kind of love." The nearest Christian to you is your husband or your wife. So the place to begin to live out Christ's love as a Christian is right there with that person who is nearest to you. And, you know, I believe that that's one of the most beautiful things I've ever seen in the kingdom of God. You don't see it too often today, but how beautiful it is when you do.

Here's a woman, for example, who in my opinion is very difficult to love, even for me as a pastor, and yet her husband loves her. He really does, and he shows that he does, steadfastly and faithfully. That's something, and vice versa. And you see that in the kingdom of God with people who aren't easy to love, and yet they go on loving them, and that is the love that excels. And that is the love that God wants us to manifest in our Christian marriages, so that these Christian marriages can be the covenant foundation of God's household and family, and so the church can be a beautiful thing in this world, because it sets before men the image of the love of Christ for the church.

We've all sinned and come short of the glory of God, but with the help of the Holy Spirit in dependence upon Christ, more and more we can know the love that excels.

May God grant it for his name's sake.

Amen.

8

Summing It Up

Song of Solomon 8:8–8:14

Congregation of the Lord Jesus, we come tonight to what I would call the summation—a summary of the great principles, the fundamental and primary principles, that God would have us learn from this wonderful song of love. So, without further introduction, I want to get into those three great principles.

The first great principle that I would put before you from this text of the Bible is what I would call *the primacy of chastity*, or, in other words, quite bluntly and simply, the importance of waiting for sex until marriage. Some Bible commentators say the bride—or the wife of Solomon—here is reminiscing about her own childhood. They say that these words are the words spoken by her brothers when she was a little child and not yet mature. And they are saying to one another, "We have a young sister, and her breasts are not yet grown. What shall we do for our sister for the day she is spoken for?" (8:8). And they say that the probability is that this girl's father died; and it's possible that her mother remarried. It's also possible that a stepfather also died, leaving the responsibility in the hands of her brothers. That would explain why they are addressed and spoken of as they are a little bit later on. It would also explain why they would have this responsibility for her.

Well, we can't be sure that this was the case, but it's a very plausible reconstruction based on the language you find in chapter 1 as well as here, where her brothers are spoken of very much as half-brothers are spoken of in the Bible. The other explanation given is that these are the words of Solomon and his wife, and they are speaking of her little sister—who was perhaps left as a responsibility to them. Again, as in many instances like this for which we do not have final answers, it doesn't really make any difference in the basic teaching. The main point remains perfectly clear, and that is the fact that God's covenant people strongly believe that sex is only proper in marriage. "We have a young sister, and her breasts are not yet grown." She's still very young, in other words, and imma-ture, yet already her guardians—whether it be these brothers or Solomon and his wife thinking about her younger sister, it doesn't matter—those who have responsibility for her are already thinking ahead to the day of her marriage, and they want her to be a virgin when that moment arrives.

So what do they do? They take stock of her personality, and they consider her traits, and they analyze her character to decide whether she is a wall or a door. If she is a *wall*—that is, if she shows in her character or in the many things that manifest the tendencies of her character—that she is very strongly determined to resist any improper advances made toward her, then they reward her with ornaments of silver. But if she is a *door*—that is, if her character doesn't manifest the needed strength and stability, and she shows herself to be all too easily subject to the advances made by men—then they say they're going to barricade her with planks of cedar.

In other words, they are going to deal with her according to the tendencies of her character as they have already begun to manifest themselves, even while she is still very young.

Now, I believe that parents can learn something of tremendous importance here, because children are incredibly different. They have the same parents; they grow up in the same home environment. And if you are like we are, I know that you do your best to give them all the same basic instruction and teaching. Yet the fact is—and it's a strange and mysterious thing—that one of them may be very strong in character, like a wall, and even when they're very young you know there's something about the character and the direction in which that young personality is going that you can trust them a great deal. They're like a wall, and you can reward that fact with ornaments of silver. But another child in the same family may manifest the very opposite tendencies of character; even while very young they seem to be weak in determination. They don't have that strong sense of resolution, and they don't have that firm sense of direction. They are like a door, open to all kinds of temptations, and we have to be alert to that fact. We have to analyze their character correctly, and we have to take measures according to what our children really are.

Nothing then could be greater folly than for parents to imagine that they can adopt one and the same pattern of discipline and training in every respect for all their children, irrespective of the differences between them. This often happens. The first one comes along, and that child's character seems to be firm. There doesn't seem to be much to worry about, and so you can have a kind of relaxed, disciplinary attitude toward that child. And the foolish parent may then just say, "Well, it worked with that one, so it's bound to work with the others." When you do that you run into all kinds of problems. And the same can be true in reverse. That first child can be a difficult one, one who shows many weaknesses in character, so you have to be very strict. But the danger is that you might be overly strict with another child whose character is not the same and whose temperament is very different. So you have three or four children, and you have to measure their character and temperament, and you have to take stock of what they are, just like these brothers or Solomon and his wife did with this little sister.

Even while she was very young, they began to analyze her character. And they said, "If she's going to be a wall, we'll deal with her this way, and if she's going to be a door, we'll deal with her that way." And so let us say you have two daughters, and one of them is like a wall and the other is like a door, what are you going to do? You're going to have to reward the one by giving that one more liberty, and you're going to have to restrict the other one with battlements of cedar. And when you do, there's going to be an outcry in that family, and that child that is the more restricted is going to cry out in pain. They're going to say, "You're not fair. You're not just." And you're going to have to bear and suffer that, and you're going to have to do the right thing regardless. You know the Bible says, "He who spares the rod hates his son" (Prov. 13:24). If you're not willing to face the music as a parent, if you're not willing to discipline, even when there's an outcry, then you can't accomplish your mission and your task as parents. I'm sure you know what happens when you don't do that. You see it in the tragic story of Eli. God says he honored his own pleasures and his own desires rather than honoring God, and we can't do that. That's not our privilege; we're supposed to honor God, and so if there's a difference, we have to take account of that difference and deal with our children differently. The sad thing is that too often we wait too long to analyze their character correctly, and we wait until they are too old to take the remedial action that these brothers did, or Solomon and his wife. And so you see in this the tremendous importance of the sanctity of sex.

I've said over and over as we've gone through this book, there is a reason in the plan of God why it is always the girl who comes in for mention. It was in order that this marriage might reflect the image of Christ and the church, and because Christ is perfect, therefore all the problems in the Song of Solomon are put in terms of the woman. But I don't think we can leave this point without emphasizing another thing, and that is that *this also applies equally to the boys.* How about our little sons—is it the same requirements that God would have us apply to them?

Well, I think we are all aware of the fact that there has been a tendency in Western culture, and even in the churches within Western culture, to adopt a kind of double standard. The Christian church, sad to say, has gone along to a lamentable extent with this, and so we say, "Of course, we expect our girls to remain pure, while it's all right for the young fellows to sow their wild oats—that's to be expected." It's nothing less than scandalous that the church of God should ever have in any way countenanced this very false and dangerous teaching. I think one of the reasons for the women's liberation movement today in Western culture is a backlash from this false double standard. If I was under a double standard where the men were allowed to do just as they please, and the women weren't, I'd rebel against it, too, because I know God is not that kind of a God. But I've got news for you. God has never said that this kind of thing was all right. God has never said, I want the girls to wait for sex until marriage, but you fellows don't have to. That's exactly what God does *not* say in his holy Word.

I want to take a detour here to point this out. I'm quoting the book of Proverbs where Solomon expresses God's

wisdom on this matter with respect to sons of the house of
Israel. He says in Proverbs 2:

> My son, if you accept my words,
>   and store up my commands within you. . . . (v. 1)

> Wisdom will enter your heart,
>   and knowledge will be pleasant to your soul.
> Discretion will protect you,
>   and understanding will guard you. (vv. 10–11)

> It will save you also from the adulteress,
>   from the wayward wife with her seductive words. (v. 16)

> For her house leads down to death,
>   and her paths to the spirits of the dead. (v. 18)

And in Proverbs 5 we read:

> My son, pay attention to my wisdom,
>   listen well to my words of insight,
> that you may maintain discretion
>   and that your lips may preserve knowledge.
> For the lips of an adulteress drip honey,
>   and her speech is smoother than oil;
> but in the end she is bitter as gall,
>   sharp as a double-edged sword.
> Her feet go down to death;
>   her steps lead straight to the grave. (vv. 1–5)

> Drink water from your own cistern,
>   running water from your own well. (v. 15)

May your fountain be blessed,
    and may you rejoice with the wife of your youth.
A loving doe, a graceful deer—
    may her breasts satisfy you always,
    may you ever be captivated by her love.
Why be captivated, my son, by an adulteress? (vv. 18–20)

A man's ways are in full view of the LORD,
    and he examines all his paths.
The evil deeds of a wicked man ensnare him;
    The cords of his sin hold him fast. (vv. 21–22)

Again in Proverbs 7:

I noticed among the young men,
    A youth who lacked judgment.
He was going down the street near her corner,
    walking along in the direction of her house
at twilight, as the day was fading, as the dark of night set in.

Then out came a woman to meet him,
    dressed like a prostitute and with crafty intent.
(She is loud and defiant,
    her feet never stay at home.) (vv. 7–11)

She took hold of him and kissed him
    and with a brazen face she said: (v. 13)

"Come, let's drink deep of love till morning;
    Let's enjoy yourselves with love [eros]!" (v. 18)

With persuasive words she led him astray;
    she seduced him with her smooth talk.

All at once he followed her
   like an ox going to the slaughter,
like a deer stepping into a noose
   till an arrow pierces his liver,
like a bird darting into a snare,
   little knowing it will cost him his life.

Now then, my sons, listen to me;
   pay attention to what I say.
Do not let your heart turn to her ways
   or stray into her paths.
Many are the victims she has brought down;
   her slain are a mighty throng.
Her house is a highway to the grave,
   leading down to the chambers of death. (vv. 21–27)

Now maybe you think that's exaggeration, but whenever
I read those passages I think of a musician I once knew—a
brilliant saxophone and clarinet player. He decided to do his
own thing, to have a life of liberated sex, so he had many
women. But as he began to grow older, he realized there was
nothing permanent in it, and he decided he wanted a wife.
So he got married, and I remember when he was married,
but you know it didn't last. How could it? He didn't realize
that he'd done something to himself, but he had. He'd done
something to himself—he had incapacitated himself for the
discipline of marriage. That's what he had done. And I still
remember the last time I met him. What a sad thing it was—
I'll never forget it. He told me he was writing love letters to
a prostitute, and she was writing love letters to him. Neither
one of them was willing to give up promiscuous sex, and yet
there was somehow that longing in them for something more
permanent. *Of course*, God doesn't agree with the double

standard, and if there is any young man here who thinks that he can have it, and she can't, he doesn't know anything about the true and living God because God has no double standard. God's standard is *wait until you're married.*

The second thing we see here in this concluding part of the Song of Solomon is *the testimony of gratitude.* For she says, "I was a wall. Yes, even when my breasts were like towers, even when I was a fully-matured, young woman, still I was like a wall. I maintained that the place for sex was in marriage." And you see this all the way through this Song. Remember how she said, "I want you to swear, daughters of Jerusalem, you're not going to tempt me. I don't want it." She was indeed like a wall, even when she was a mature woman. And she says, precisely because of this, "Then I became in his eyes as one who found peace" (8:10 NKJV). And there you have a beautiful play on words in the Hebrew language because the word for Solomon is built on the root of the word for *peace—shalom.* That's when she found peace—when she found Solomon. And she found him because that's the kind of girl that Solomon wanted. That's the kind of woman any man wants. That's true no matter how promiscuous he's been. I knew of a man brought up in the Reformed faith, and he went off on this same path of sexual liberation, but then when he got a little older and got tired of it all, do you know what he wanted? Sure, he wanted a virgin. Of course. He wanted exactly the kind of woman that you have described here in the Song of Songs. Of course, he didn't meet that standard himself, but never mind, that's what he wants.

You can't help but wonder if these brothers of the Shulamite weren't a little too strict with her. If she was a wall, why didn't they reward her with the battlements of silver? Why did they have her working off there in the vineyard like a slave as she tells us back in chapter 1, when she says her brothers were angry and they made her take care of the vine-yard? It certainly was possible that they erred, seriously, on the side of strictness. That's why Paul warns fathers not to exasperate their children, not to go too far in the direction of strictness of discipline. But even so, even if her brothers were too strict—since she was a wall, they didn't need to deal with her that way—still, *now*, she recognizes the good in it. They had her working down there in the vineyard, and it was probably Solomon's vineyard, and they were probably stewards in Solomon's vineyard, and that's how she met him. And while she recognizes that they were perhaps too strict in their discipline, she also realizes they had the right motive, and *now* she's thankful for it.

She uses a beautiful illustration to tell us this; she says, "Solomon had a vineyard in Baal Hamon" (8:11 NKJV), and that's probably where they met and where her family earned their livelihood taking care of that vineyard for Solomon. And they had to give Solomon a thousand shekels of silver for his fruit; they had to give him the lion's share, and they had what was left over. But that was only right, because it was Solomon's vineyard. Well, she says, "I've got a vineyard too, and now I'm giving it to Solomon." And she says, "I give a thousand to him," and in the Bible a thousand is the number for fullness. "I give my whole self, all I am I give to Solomon, but," she says, "don't forget this. I also give the two hundred shekels for those who took care of it." And that means that there is in her heart an undying sense of gratitude to those very brothers who were so jealous to protect her purity. Now she is thankful for them. Maybe she wasn't at the time; maybe she was really grieved when she was down there in the vine-yard working away, not near any young man who she had her eye on, but now she's thankful.

And I think we parents need to remember this, too. You

know the Bible says, "No discipline seems pleasant at the time" (Heb. 12:11), and that's certainly true of children. You will never devise discipline that your children will enjoy—you may as well forget it. Discipline that children will enjoy has never been invented. No chastening for the present seems to be joyful, that's what the book of Hebrews says, so you're going to have to accept the fact that it's going to be unpleasant, and the children aren't going to like it. But that doesn't matter, if one day they look back and thank you for it, if they say, "Thank you, Dad. Boy, what misery it was at the time, but thank you." When they lookback at the time and say, "I thought I really hated you at the time, Mother, but now I realize that I really love you for what you did." That's the reward you'll have if you do what the Bible says. If you don't do what the Bible says to do, you won't have that reward, but if you do what the Bible says, you will.

I've experienced it myself. I remember when I was bringing up our children, and they wanted to go dancing. I said, "No, you can't go dancing." And my kids were always the kind who wanted a biblical answer, so they said, "Where do you get that in the Bible?" So I said, "It's in the book of Exodus." "Where in the book of Exodus?" "Exodus 20." "Where Exodus 20?" "In verse 12" (which is the fifth commandment). Well, that finally stopped them: "Honor your father and your mother." I said, "That's it. You've got to honor me, and I say you can't go dancing." Well, they couldn't get out of that, so they had to bow to it. And there was grief in our house. But I've been thanked since. It took a few years, but I've been thanked since for that discipline, and that's exactly what you parents will get some day. But you've got to face the music now, and deal with the problem in the way that God says to deal with it.

So, here you see the beautiful harmony in the teaching of

the Bible. What seems at first sight to be contradictory is not really contradictory. The Bible says, "You are to leave your father and mother, and you are to cleave to your wife"—give her the thousand. But it also says, "Honor your father and your mother." Is that a contradiction? Not at all. You give the thousand to your husband or wife, but you give two hundred to your dad and mother. You give yourself and all you are to that husband, but you don't forget to love your parents, and you don't forget to be grateful to them for what they've done to you. I certainly thank my parents today for the discipline I had. It wasn't perfect—but I thank God for it because I know if there's any good in me today I owe a lot of it to the fact that *they* faced the music and gave me that discipline.

Are you thankful to God for these things, young people? You probably don't feel very thankful. But as soon as you start to think in a biblical way you're going to be thankful. You're going to say, "I'm so thankful for parents that are different from all those around us in the world today, who just let their kids do anything. I thank God I've got parents who say, 'No, you can't,' and even if I go up and down the room and cry, they still say, 'No, you can't do it.'" That's what you ought to be saying. You ought to be thankful that your parents have sat down and talked with you and disciplined you, and sometimes did things you didn't like at all because that's what brings the peaceable fruits of righteousness, as the Bible says, in those that have been exercised by it. And that's exactly what this woman did.

So she comes to the end of the Song and says, "Number one on the agenda: *Wait until you're married for sex.* Number two on the agenda: *Be thankful to those who have pounded that into you and have tried to safeguard that in you, because it's that important!*" And finally we go on to the third and last point. And, you know, it's not easy to describe exactly in words what this is all about, but let me attempt it. It's what I would call *a kind of longing and yearning that remains in the heart of those who have known the love that God intended them to know in marriage.* Let's hear how it is put here. He says:

> You who dwell in the gardens
>   with friends in attendance,
> let me hear your voice! (8:13)

And she answers back:

> Make haste, my lover,
>   and be like a gazelle
> or like a young stag
>   on the spice-laden mountains. (8:14)

Now if you've read the book carefully, you'll remember that that's almost like the language they were speaking to each other before they got married. It's the language of yearning and longing that arises from some unfulfilled desire. And some Bible commentators say this means that when a marriage is blessed by God and done in God's way, there's going to be a kind of constant renewal of love, like a continual courtship. And there is certainly truth in that thesis. The nearer our marriages approximate the great divine example, the more they're going to be like that. There will always be something new and fresh in that romance of marriage, and we ought to seek that. God can give it to us.

But I'm convinced that there's something more here than this, because when the Bible tells us to love our wives the way Christ loved the church, and for wives to love their husbands the way the church loves Christ, he is setting before us a kind of love that has two aspects in tension. The two aspects are, first, *the present realization of love between Christ and his church.* And the Bible says we *are* the Bride of Christ if we are a church made up of believers. Paul says, "I promised you to one husband" (2 Cor. 11:2), and he is the Lord Jesus. So the church *already* is the bride of Christ. But the second aspect is *what lies ahead at Christ's second coming.* And that means that there is a longing in the heart of the church for that ultimate perfection. That great day when we will be with Christ in a way that far transcends what we know in the present.

And in marriage, too—for Christian believers—there is a realization that finality and perfection is not to be found in this earthly life. What I'm saying, in other words, is that anyone who has been married—even if they've had a good Christian marriage that goes God's way right from the beginning—will realize if they are honest and biblical that their marriage isn't the ultimate thing. You read some of the literature of the world you might think it was. Romanticism almost puts marriage in the place of an idol, but we must never view it in that way. The Bible says God has put eternity in the heart of man, and that the heart is never going rest in anything as fleeting as marriage. *Eros* doesn't last long, does it? It's a momentary and fleeting thing. It can never satisfy the eternity that God has set in your heart. Even companionship will only last for a little while. One poet put it like this:

> She lived unknown, and few could know
> When Lucy ceased to be;
> But she is in her grave, and, oh,
> The difference to me!

Even the love of companionship is temporal, and because God has put eternity in our hearts, nothing will ever satisfy our ultimate need except that which is eternal. And we're not going to find that in marriage because the Bible says, "At the resurrection people will neither marry nor be given in marriage" (Matt. 22:30). Marriage belongs to this present temporal order. It's like the leaf that fades away or the grass of the field that perishes, and we can never find our ultimate joy and satisfaction in it.

And that's why the Bible says, "Those who have wives should live as if they had none" (1 Cor. 7:29). Did you ever think about the people who aren't married? If marriage was intended to be the ultimate thing, what about them? Why, we'd have to say they missed out because they don't have the ultimate thing. But that's not what the Bible says. If there are any of you here that aren't married—and are not even destined to be married—that doesn't mean you miss out, not at all, because marriage is not the ultimate thing. You won't obtain the ultimate thing just because you are married. No, it's something that goes beyond marriage; it has to be. And what is it? It's the consummation of the great marriage between Christ and his church. Everything else is fleeting and momentary and changing. So, even if you have a beautiful marriage, like the two people here in this song, you must learn from all the imperfections in it. Anyone here want to deny that? Anyone here have the perfect marriage? Anyone here have the marriage that is without any tears? Stand up. Of course, you don't, and God is teaching you by that. It's *not* the ultimate thing. *Nothing in this world is the ultimate thing.* The ultimate thing is to be found only in Jesus Christ, and the great and eternal marriage of Christ and the church.

Maybe you may have noticed how in all the stories that the fiction writers write they always speak of living "happily ever after." Well, that doesn't happen. Many of the love songs of our culture talk about loving "forever and a day," but there is no forever and a day for earthly marriages; that's not to be because God has ordained that we should find our fullness only in him. If you're trying to find it in your marriage, you're not going to find it, because it's not there. So your marriage hasn't really reached its objective unless, in that marriage, you turn your face not only to each other, but even more together to God. And you become "heirs together of the grace of life" (1 Peter 3:7 NKJV), and you say, "We're going to seek the kingdom of God together. Hand in hand we're going to seek the kingdom of our Lord and Savior, Jesus Christ," and then when your love is caught up in a love that is far greater, marriage reaches its ultimate meaning in the transcendent glory of the kingdom of Christ.

To die is to be with Christ, and—for believers—to die is gain (Phil. 1:21). And two Christian people, when they really come to know what life is all about, look at it that way. More and more their faces are turned to the Lord Jesus Christ and his covenant promise. That's why the Bible says we are to be "heirs together of the grace of life," seeking the kingdom of God and his righteousness first, remembering that the chief end of man is not to have a happy marriage but to glorify God and to enjoy him forever. And that is why there always is this profound sense of longing—this sense of unfulfilled perfection—at the heart of every truly Christian marriage. And it's not until a husband and wife realize that the ultimate is not to be found in each other, but only in their God, their Creator and Savior, that they finally reach the end for which even this Song was written, because the church has always recognized in the last few words of this song a kind of echo of the words that we also find at the end the Bible: "Even so, come, Lord Jesus!" (Rev. 22:20 NKJV). When our heart beats in tune with the heart of God, we all become the bride of Jesus. That is why we can't help but cry out, "Even so, come, Lord Jesus." And when that happens we will finally have that which is final; then we will know the ultimate rapture in the perfect marriage.

May God grant us the wisdom and strength to make our marriages here on earth a means to that final glory.

Amen.

Also from P&R Publishing

People debate whether Song of Songs is an allegory or a romantic manual. Duguid goes beyond this, showing a focus on Christ that has profound gospel application for all Christians.

The Reformed Expository Commentary (REC) series is accessible to both pastors and lay readers. Each volume in the series provides exposition that gives careful attention to the biblical text, is doctrinally Reformed, focuses on Christ through the lens of redemptive history, and applies the Bible to our contemporary setting.

Praise for the Reformed Expository Commentary Series

"Well-researched and well-reasoned, practical and pastoral, shrewd, solid, and searching."
—**J. I. Packer**

"A rare combination of biblical insight, theological substance, and pastoral application."
—**Al Mohler**

"Here, rigorous expository methodology, nuanced biblical theology, and pastoral passion combine."
—**R. Kent Hughes**